Integrating Programming, Evaluation and Participation in Design

First published in 1992, this book is about making connections that may lead towards a new professionalism, since the past several decades have given rise mainly to new kinds of specialists in the areas of programming, evaluation, and participation. The implications for such integration are far reaching, with profound future effects on the physical environment, the design professions, and the education of designers. The book is split into four sections dealing with facility programming, several forms of evaluation, participatory design, and the application of Theory Z principles. This book will be of interest to students of architecture and design.

Integrating Programming, Evaluation and Participation in Design

A Theory Z Approach

Henry Sanoff

First published in 1992
by Routledge

This edition first published in 2016 by Routledge
2 Park Square, Milton Park, Abingdon, Oxon, OX14 4RN
and by Routledge
711 Third Avenue, New York, NY 10017

Routledge is an imprint of the Taylor & Francis Group, an informa business

© 1992 Henry Sanoff

The right of Henry Sanoff to be identified as author of this work has been asserted by him in accordance with sections 77 and 78 of the Copyright, Designs and Patents Act 1988. All rights reserved. No part of this book may be reprinted or reproduced or utilised in any form or by any electronic, mechanical, or other means, now known or hereafter invented, including photocopying and recording, or in any information storage or retrieval system, without permission in writing from the publishers.

Publisher's Note
The publisher has gone to great lengths to ensure the quality of this reprint but points out that some imperfections in the original copies may be apparent.

Disclaimer
The publisher has made every effort to trace copyright holders and welcomes correspondence from those they have been unable to contact.

A Library of Congress record exists under LC control number: 92029044

ISBN 13: 978-1-138-20338-9 (hbk)
ISBN 13: 978-1-315-47173-0 (ebk)
ISBN 13: 978-1-138-20339-6 (pbk)

Integrating Programming, Evaluation and Participation in Design

A theory Z approach

HENRY SANOFF
North Carolina State University

Avebury
Aldershot · Brookfield USA · Hong Kong · Singapore · Sydney

© Henry Sanoff 1992

All rights reserved. No part of this publication may be reproduced, stored in a retrieval system, or transmitted in any form or by any means, electronic, mechanical, photocopying, recording or otherwise without the prior permission of the publisher.

Published by
Avebury
Ashgate Publishing Limited
Gower House, Croft Road
Aldershot, Hants GU11 3HR
England

Ashgate Publishing Company
Old Post Road
Brookfield, Vermont 05036
USA

A CIP catalogue record for this book is avaialble from the British Library and the US Library of Congress.

ISBN 1 85628 338 0

Printed and Bound in Great Britain by
Athenaeum Press Ltd., Newcastle upon Tyne.

Contents

Foreword

Professionals are not known by what thay do, but by the way they do it. Professionalism lies in expertise and expertise relies on skill, method, and knowledge. While many areas of design such as architecture, landscape architecture, and interior design are established professions, much of what professionals do, have been and will continue to be done by lay people. Experience and knowledge resides with lay people as much as with experts. In fact, humanity has done without design professionals for a long time, and probably would continue to survive in their absence.

While designers have thought of the built environment as dependent upon them, it is becoming increasingly evident that their decision domain is shrinking. This is partially explained by the designers neglect in being sufficiently responsive to human needs. It is clear that designers cannot be responsible for everything, nor can they control everything. Yet, it is apparent that the role of the professional is continually being questioned, as is the issue of human accountability as it has been practiced. Creating environments that are more responsive to human needs will require changes in traditional practice. Practice in the future promises to offer new challenges, since the role of the professional will need to be multi-faceted. Designers will require new skills and knowledge as an enabler, technical advisor, social worker, and bureaucratic trouble-shooter. Learning how to listen, not only to the paying client, but to people who use and are effected by the environment, within the social and historic context, can produce a professional with an expanded capacity for shaping the future. Habraken (1986) envisions this new role, not only to study the health and well-being of the physical environment, but to help it become better through design intervention.

This book is about making connections that may lead towards a new professionalism, since the past several decades have given rise mainly to new kinds of specialists in the areas of programming, evaluation, and participation. The implications for such an integration are far reaching, with profound future effects on the physical environment, the design professions, and the education of designers.

1 Facility programming

Programming is generally viewed as an information processing system setting out design directions that will accommodate the needs of the user, the client, the designer, or the developer. The nature and scope of design decisions and design information have changed rapidly, and the role of programming has thus changed as well. The uses of programming have been extended from primarily acquiring and organizing information (Heimsath, 1977) to investigating and developing information, analyzing client and user needs, and evaluating projects after construction and occupancy (Freidman, Zimring, & Zube, 1978; Wener, 1989).

Programming has been seen as a valuable resource for a systematized process that provides a structured framework for accumulating and classifying data. As an analytical process, it encourages decision making through objective procedures rather than on individual assumptions or personal prejudices. A report by the Building Research Board of the National Research Ciouncil (1986) on programming practices states that 'programming services may not always result in new construction or changes to the physical building, but in organizational or managerial changes that achieve the same objectives' (p.1).

There is considerable diversity in the use of the terms *space programming, facility programming, and functional programming* and in their meaning within the design professions. In addition to the differing terms that identify programming, there are also philosophical differences regarding the

An earlier version of this paper was first published in Zube, E.H. & Moore, G.T. (eds.), 1989, *Advances in Environment, Behavior, and Design*, Plenum, New York.

of *programming*. Expressions such as 'programming is design, programming is not design,' and 'programming is getting ready for design,' underlie the diversity of purposes and places of programming in the design process.

Everyone, however, would accept the view that a program is the organized collection of specific information that involves developing, managing, and communicating. Most will also agree that programming is the process of identifying and defining the needs of a facility. Although general features have emerged, programming should be recognized as a dynamic and interactive process.

The basic references for programming lie in the published volumes of Palmer (1981), Pena (1977), Preiser (1978, 1985, 1992), Sanoff (1978), and White (1972). The principal objective of Preiser's edited collection *Facility Programming* (1978) and *Programming the Built Environment* (1985) is to provide an authoritative overview of the user-oriented programming approaches that are currently to be found at work in architectural and environmental design. Both books describe the professional programming activity conducted by architectural and programming firms. The topics covered range from problem definition, cross cultural programming, and post-occupancy evaluation to adaptive reuse and other more specific examples of programming. Each chapter is largely self-contained and represents various attitudes about programming and about the breadth, scope, and prospects of the field.

As a complement to the Preiser volumes, Sanoff's *Methods of Architectural Programming* (1978) is about the technical aspects of programming. Here the material moves from data-gathering techniques, through methods of synthesizing and organizing data, to a field application of programming techniques that makes use of user expertise. The volume stresses a general flexibility of approach, in which the techniques may be combined and merged, depending on the situation on hand.

Palmer's *Architects Guide to Facility Programming* (1981) covers much of the same ground as the Preiser and Sanoff volumes, though attempts to integrate information-gathering techniques with case studies. Although it was written 3 years latter than Sanoff's book, it fails to show the development of facility evaluation studies and their relationship to facility programming.

By contrast, Pena's *Problem Seeking* (1977) is a presentation of one approach, the CRS (Caudill, Rowlett, and Scott, Architects and Planners) method of programming. The five-step process is presented in lock-step fashion with partially worked examples. Rather than adopting a flexible attitude toward the organization of information, the book views the role of the programmer as being conformity to a predetermined format.

In an effort to bridge the theory-practice gap, White (1982) conducted interviews with architects to assess their attitudes toward programming practice. In an open-ended telephone survey of 73 architects in the United States, programming strengths were described by the respondents as including 'thorough rigorous analytic process, strong client/user participation, programming tailored to each project, strong integration with design and successful projects, and happy clients.' The recurring programming problems were reported to be 'finding the true needs of the client, getting clients to make decisions, and clients don't appreciate programming at program-design connection' (p.37).

According to White (1983), clients are frequently unaware of their needs and sometimes are impatient or do not understand why the information is needed. Some clients will not permit the staff to participate in the programming process. There are also occasions when the client says one thing and the programmer hears another; the client often faces difficult choices and is not prepared to work as quickly as the process requires. These difficulties cited by practitioners clearly suggest the need for considerable improvement in communication with the client, as well as collaborative involvement in the programming process.

When asked about the reasons for offering programming services, beyond providing a better building, the respondents in the White study said that such a service 'facilitates the design process, marketing, project management tool, client confidence in project and firm, and saves client and firm time and money' (p.52). The majority of architects agreed that programming provided the client a way to participate in the project's planning process. They also indicated that programming leads to improvements in the client's operation; therefore, programming firms sometimes serve also as management consultants. Hellmuth, Obata & Kassabaum (Silver & Klein, 1985) described the programming process as being able to 'promote confidence, teamwork and consensus; convey a sense of care and attention to users; minimize space-allocation abuses; and leave a clear trail of decisions and approvals for superiors to review' (p.3).

Comparing programming models

Architectural programming is not a rigidly defined process. Each programmer has his or her style and emphasis, and each project requires a certain amount of custom fitting of any model that a programmer may have. Because a number of programmers have described their approach, the purpose of this section is to examine seven of these approaches, to compare their similarities and differences, and to combine them into a composite model.

The seven models

The models reviewed are by Davis & Szigetti (1979), Farbstein (in Palmer, 1981, p.33), Kurtz(in Preiser, 1978, p.41), McLaughlin (1976, p.42), Moleski (in Palmer, 1981, p.37), Pena (1977, p.43), and White (1972, p.44). These authors were selected because their programming work is documented in the literature and they follow a well-delineated process.

Gerald Davis. Davis's programming model (Davis & Szigetti, 1979) is a 21 step process (Figure1.1) that begins with preprogramming and moves through evaluating the facility in use. It is directed toward the planning of corporate facilities. The first part of the process, as with Moleski and Kurtz (below), is to become familier with the client's business organization, operation, activities, and needs, both present and long range. The programming steps include gathering data on the operating facilities; on physiological needs, such as those affecting health, safety, and performance; and on behavioral requirements, such as those affecting motivation, learning, and attitudes. The impact of the project is evaluated in terms of its effect on the functioning of the organization as well as its effect on the community and the environment. Cost estimates are made, and essential criteria for design are established. Throughout the design process, the programmer provides feedback to the designer. After the facility is built, the programmer assists management in moving into the facilities, and in their fine tuning. The facilities are evaluated after they have been in use for a period of time, usually within 6 months.

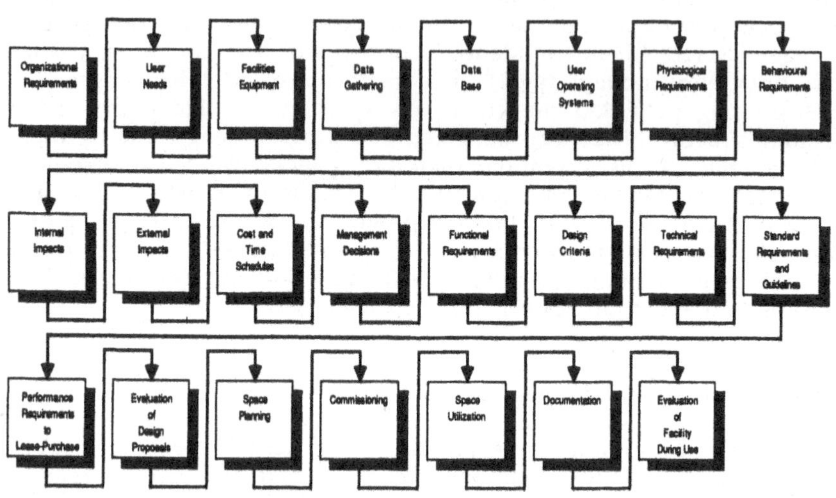

Figure 1.1 Davis's programming process

Jay Farbstein. Farbstein's process (Palmer, 1981) consistes of five steps (Figure 1.2) that identify client needs. His first step is to search the existing literature for information on the building type. The next step is to identify the users of the facility and their activities, attitudes, and characteristics. Then performance criteria are established for area needs, circulation, ambient environment, safety and security, surfaces, finishes, flexibility, and site design. After the client reviews the performance criteria, the design issues are identified, the program options are identified for each issues, and each option is measured in terms of costs, benefits, and trade-offs. The client is consulted again to assess the options. Space specifications and adjacency relationships are developed. Finally, the client is consulted once more for approval of the program and the budget. Farbstein's recent work (1985) stresses the periodic assessment of the facility's performance after occupancy.

Kaplan, McLaughlin, Diaz (KMD). McLaughlin (1976) of KMD believes that programming is design, and that evaluation is an integral part of the design process. KMD's programming procedure consists of three phases (Figure 1.3), the first of which includes identification of the user, the user's organizational philosophy and objectives, and the financial feasibility of the project. The second phase considers the client's openness to new ideas, the physical context, a functional analysis, and aesthetic demands; this phase includes a survey of building types and all factors that may influence the form and content of the building. The final phase corresponds more closely to what is typically referred to as *project development,* in which studies of building organization, schedules, outline specifications, and budgets are conducted. McLaughlin and KMD also follow a three-phase process of evaluating their buildings that begins in the programming stage of the project, with an exploration of the future occupants' expectations of the new facility. After the building has been occupied for several months, another survey of user expectations is conducted. The third survey of the users occurs after they have adjusted their work processes to the new facility.

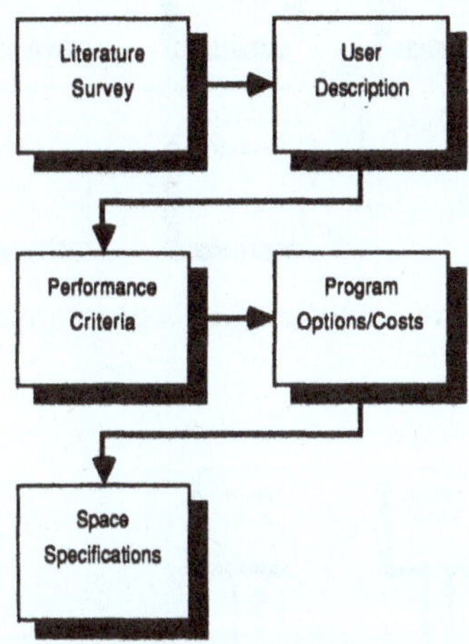

Figure 1.2 Farbstein's programming process

John M. Kurtz. The programming model presented by Kurtz (Preiser, 1978) emphasizes iterative programming, which continues into the design phase (Figure 1.4). Kurtz's belief is that generalized long-range programmatic decisions should be made at the beginning of a building project. The first step in this model, as in that of Moleski (below), is for the programmer to be familiar with the client's operation, philosophy, and objectives. The basic program includes a literature search on the building type, a determination of the client's operating requirements, and a preliminary program of the building's organization, space sizes, and relationships. The basic program is presented to the client for feedback, and the program is revised and presented again until general agreement is reached. The design phase is considered part of the programming process because the client continues to provide feedback in reviews and revisions of preliminary designs.

Walter H. Moleski. Moleski's approach (Palmer, 1981) consistes of four stages and two intermediate reviews with the client, the architect, and the programmer (Figure 1.5). The activities are (1) awareness; (2) diagnosis: (3) first review; (4) strategy; (5) second review; and (6) action. Initial familiarity with the client's operation occurs in Step 1, through reviews with the client and through interviewing the client to determine the nature of the organ-

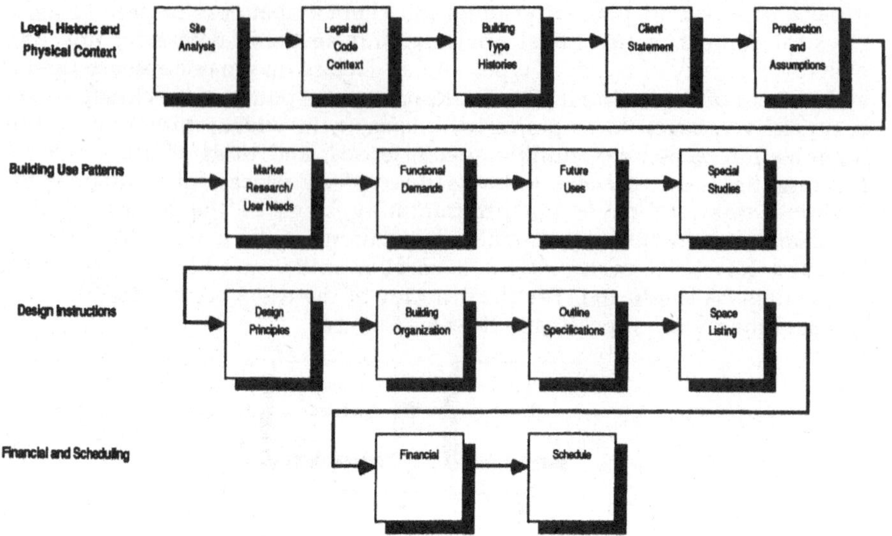

Figure 1.3 McLaughlin's programming process

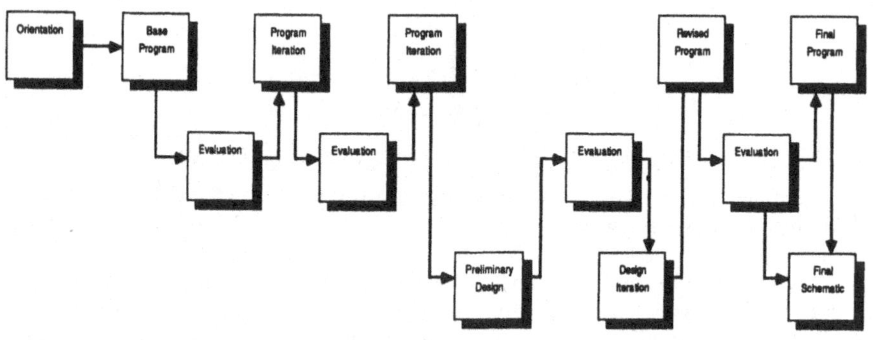

Figure 1.4 Kurtz's programming process

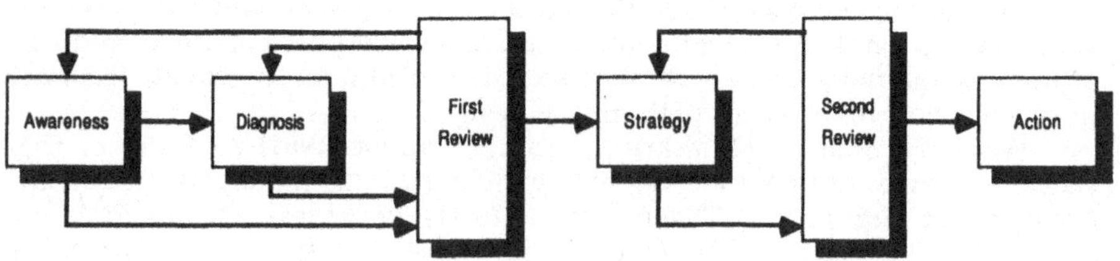

Figure 1.5 Moleski's programming process

ization, its functions, and its satisfactions and dissatisfactions with the present facility. Problem areas are identified, about which information is to be gathered. Information is then gathered in Step 2 through the use of such techniques as interviews, observations, and questionnaires. The information gathered is analyzed to show activities, relationships, problems, and needs. The data are organized, and concepts are formulated in a preliminary program that constitutes the awareness and diagnosis stages of the process. The first review, which occurs in Step 3 in the process, is a meeting with the client to discuss the preliminary problem statement, and concepts and to select concepts for further development. The fourth step is to develop a strategy or to establish performance criteria. A more specific set of design needs is identified, and recommendations are made to the designer con- cerning spatial characteristics, physical conditions, symbolic attributes, and spatial arrangements. The second review (Step 5) is a client meeting to discuss the recommended program, to establish the architectural intent of the facility, and to obtain final approval of the program. The programmer's responsibilities extend into the action or follow-up stage, in which he or she consults with the designer on the intent of the program and evaluates the design solutions.

William T. Pena of CRS, Inc. Pena's programming procedure (1977) developed for CRS, is a comprehensive process of five steps: (1) establishing goals; (2) collecting facts; (3) uncovering concepts; (4) determining needs; and (5) defining the problem through a consideration of the five determinants of design: function, form, economy, time, and energy (Figure 1.6). A total of more than 132 considerations covers many aspects of a project such as the reason for the project, space requirements, and site analysis. According to Pena, programming reduces the guesswork of designing for the user's needs and seeks rather than solves design problems. The process incorporates work sessions that bring together all parties involved in the project for a specific length of time. These sessions have been referred to as the 'squatters technique' because they occur in the clients backyard. The programming squatters use graphic analysis cards and 'brown' sheets as working tools to determine the space program. The brown sheets indicate the space needs, which have been derived from the project goals, from facts, and from concepts. They represent area requirements, and serve as worksheets during work sessions. The analysis card technique is a method of graphically recording the information that must be discussed, decided upon, and sometimes discarded during the programming phase of the project. A formal presentation of the program is made to the client, with a wall display of the analysis cards and the brown sheets.

Edward T. White. White's programming method (1972) consists of a series of tasks divided into three phases: preprogramming, programming, and postprogramming (Figure 1.7). In preprogramming, the client and the programmer agree on the process, the rules, the responsibilities, and the content of the program. Any previous work on the project is collected and organized. The information to be gathered is identified, the gathering sequence is decided on, and a team is put together, each member being assigned certain tasks. The programming stage consists of information gathering, analyzing, evaluating, correlating, organizing, and documenting. The information is then submitted to the client for review and approval. Space needs are tested against the budget, and planning and design implications (which are reviewed with the client) are drawn. Directives for the designer and alternative organizational concepts for the building are formulated, and are again reviewed with the owner. Postprogramming is concerned with producing and distributing the program document and with giving presentations of the program, if appropriate.

Comparison of the seven models

All seven models make explicit the steps of collecting, analyzing, and documenting facts in a written program for the owner's approval and the designer's use. Pena described this process as collecting and analyzing facts and stating the problem. McLaughlin referred to actual and assumed needs and their characteristics. White referred to programming, and Moleski considered the steps of diagnosis and collecting, analyzing, and organizing data. Kurtz made less of a point of data collection; yet, it is understood as being part of orientation and the base program. Davis referred to selective data gathering and data bases for facilities.

Five of the programmers made a point of identifying needs relevant to the budget. Pena located economic considerations under the 'determine needs' step, and McLaughlin's economic consideration is described as financial feasibility, and occurs during various stages in the process. In his programming section, White (in Palmer, 1981) stated, 'Test space needs against budget' (p.40). Davis included three cost statements, under costs, elapsed time, and schedules, and he referred to cost again in discussing the functional requirements at each stage. Farbstein (in Palmer, 1981, p.34) outlined, 'program options and cost' to 'measure costs/benefits/trade-offs of options' and 'review cost effectiveness of options,' and his final step is for the client to approve the budget.

Another stage in the process in which there appears to be author agreement is the owner review, revision, and approval of the program. Although Pena's programming steps do not mention this topic, his brown sheets and analysis cards are used for this purpose. In his programming phase, White (in Palmer, 1981) mentioned that one should 'submit information to sources for review and approval,' 'recycle allowable space information back to sources,' 'review planning asssumptions with client,' and finally, 'review total program with client' (pp.40-41). One of Moleski's major characteristics is review, during which the client discusses the preliminary problem statement and the solution concepts, reviews the recommended program, and finally, may revise the program during the design phase. Kurtz (in Preiser, 1978, p.140) also emphasized review in his category 'iterative programming,' where the client provides feedback and 'revision of program until general agreement is reached.' 'Design-as-feedback' is devoted to changing the program during the design phase. Davis was less concerned with review; however, in his step 'evaluation of design proposals,' he did provide feedback to the design team. Farbstein had the client reviewing after performance criteria, and after program option and costs, and finally approving the program and the budget.

Although the main objective of any building program is to establish goals, only five of the authors made this an explicit step. Pena's first steps deal with establishing such goals as the accommodation of privacy or group interaction, the desired use of the existing facilities on the site, return on investment, and historic preservation. Moleski (in Palmer, 1981, p.37) was explicit only after his second review, when he said, 'establish architectural intent of the project.' Kurtz (in Preiser, 1978) started out his first step, orientation, by saying, 'determine project objectives' (p.139). Farbstein identified user objectives for the facility in his user description step, which appears to be the most comprehensive analysis of the users' social and behavioral characteristics, although McLaughlin and Davis also sought a thorough understanding of user characteristics.

There is much less consensus on what other steps are important. Two of the programmers (McLaughlin and White) believe that it is important to start the programming process by planning the program in which the objectives of the program are defined; the programming team is assembled, roles are defined, and responsibilities are assigned; information sources are identified; and a schedule is worked out.

Moleski, Kurtz, McLaughlin, and Davis have directed their methods toward the programming of organizations. They made a point of the programmer's understanding the nature, philosophy, and image of the client, its communication processes, its business plans, and its satisfactions and dissatisfactions with the present facility (Kaplan & McLaughlin,1981).

Another important function of the program is to develop design concepts, but not all of the programmers made a specific point of this. Pena devotes 34 steps to uncovering and testing concepts dealing with function, form, economy, time, and energy, and McLaughlin devotes his whole third programming phase to project development. In his programming phase, White extracts planning and design implications, sets up directives for the designer, and designs alternative organizational concepts for the building. As part of diagnosis, Moleski organizes data to discover and develop concepts for the solution of problems and the satisfaction of client needs; then, after the first review, the programmer selects concepts for further development. Farbstein identifies design issues and develops program options for each issue.

Only McLaughlin and Davis are concerned with assessing the impact of the project. Davis examines the internal impact on the functioning of the organization and its operating systems and procedures, as well as the external impact on the public that the building will serve, the surrounding community, and the natural ecology. This factor clearly advances facilities programming toward a new level of responsibility for the designer and the client.

Finally, very few of the programs studied regarded anything beyond the design of the building as being part of the programming process except Davis, who considered it the responsibility of the programmer to assist management and the users to move smoothly into the new facility, to fine-tune at move-in, and to follow up with the users or the occupants as required. Davis planted the seeds of facility management, which is a concern about the operation of a facility beyond its initial occupancy. He also regarded an evaluation of the facility during its use as being part of the programming process. He evaluates the building in terms of its original context, purpose, and requirements and in terms of the context and purposes currently applicable to its use. Evaluation is also an integral aspect of the McLaughlin process; a good part of this early evaluation work was conducted by the Environmental Analysis Group, a firm headed by Davis. Both Farbstein's and Moleski's work lend additional support to facility evaluation.

Composite programming model

Clearly, the form, description, and emphasis of each of these programming models differ. Some programmers view the programming process as being distinct from the design process, and others view it as being part of a continuing and iterative process, of which design is a part. Regardless of whether programming is considered separate from, or integral to the design, the intent of each programming model is to outline the categories of information to be collected, analyzed, and organized to assist in the design of a facility. If all seven of these models are combined into one, the result is a series of steps ranging from preprogramming to an evaluation of the facility in use. The following is a composite of these models, with a listing of each step referred to by each author (Figure 1.8).

The composite programming model is an attempt to distill and integrate the contributions of each approach. Although the model is organized sequentially in eight steps, the process is iterative and is not linear. The combined views do represent significant advances beyond each model, and they also categorically identify many key issues.

No doubt, there are programming approaches other than those identified (Davis & Szigetti, 1986). Of particular importance is the work of Gould (1986), Stone, Marraccini, and Patterson (1985), and Preiser (1985). However, their focus and contributions lie in the techniques of information organization, management, and designer-client interactions.

Robinson and Weeks (1984) whose work is more theoretical than those of the previous practitioners, argued that programming and design should be linked in an iterative process, and that any separation may result in the premature definition of a problem. By incorporating a 'hypothesis' approach, in which images are generated to be 'proved' or disproved, these authors believed, formal ideas can be included in the early stages of the programming process. The combination of verbal and graphic exploration (Figure 1.9) is intended to allow the exploration of physical form and its implications. The process requires that the design ideas be challenged and explored at their inception and throughout the stages of the design process.

Although the work of Robinson and Weeks has not been tested in practice, the architectural firm of Hellmuth, Obata & Kassalbaum (HOK) advocates a similar integrated approach (Figure 1.10), in which program and design development occur simultaneously. Although programming strategies are apt to vary with different project requirements, HOK programmers prepare clearly articulate work plans for each project.

The hypothesis approach is not unique to the field of architecture. Noted economist Downs (1976) advanced the idea of using arbitrary, but bold and imaginative, judgements and assumptions in analyzing behavior patterns and in formulating social policies. He asserted that extremely arbitrary - even

	Davis	Farbstein	KMD	Kurtz	Moleski	Pena	White
Plan The Program							
Identify participants & organize programming team	●	●	●		●	●	●
Identify programming objectives	●	●	●	●	●	●	●
Identify program context	●	●	●		●		●
Identify information needed	●	●	●	●	●	●	●
Define with client - process, sequence, tasks, schedules, rules, responsibilities	●	●	●		●		●
Identify primary information sources	●	●	●			●	●
Understand Client's Organization & Philosophy							
Nature of organization, image & philosophy	●	●		●	●		
Organization function & communication process	●	●		●	●		
Satisfaction & dissatisfaction with present facility	●	●	●		●		
Identify user objectives	●	●	●		●		
Establish Project Goals							
Functional goals	●	●		●		●	
Form related goals						●	
Economic goals	●	●				●	
Time related goals						●	
Organizing Information Search							
Collect & organize project related facts	●	●	●		●		●
Questionnaires & interviews	●	●	●	●	●	●	●
Literature search	●	●	●	●	●	●	●
Observation of existing operations & facilities	●	●	●		●		
Background information from client	●	●	●		●		●
Review similar building types & operations	●	●	●	●	●	●	
Collect facts related to building function	●	●	●	●	●	●	●
Collect facts related to building form	●	●	●	●	●	●	
Collect facts related to building economy	●	●	●			●	●
Collect facts related to time (historical, present, future)	●	●					
Analyzing Information							
Analyze collected facts	●	●	●		●		●
Functional space standards	●	●					
Tabulation of space requirements	●	●	●	●			
Spatial diagrams		●	●		●		
Interaction patterns among activities		●	●	●	●		
Written description of functional units	●	●	●		●		
Conceptual Development							
Uncover, test & develop conceptual alternatives	●	●	●		●		●
Develop functional concepts			●			●	●
Develop form, economy & time related concepts						●	
Identify Budget Related Problems & Needs							
Functional needs	●	●			●	●	●
Form needs		●			●	●	
Economic needs	●	●				●	●
Project Impact							
Impact on client's organization & operation	●						
Community & ecological impact	●						
Program review and revision	●	●	●	●	●	●	●

Figure 1.8 Composite programming model: A listing of the procedural steps used by seven programmers

ridiculous-simplifying judgements are often useful in advancing perception, analysis, or prescription. This approach clearly has its parallels in facility programming, especially in the approaches advanced by Robinson and Weeks (1984). Examples of this approach in practice have been effectively introduced by this author in the planning of numerous facilities, where ideas about building form have been developed simultaneously with building function. This approach clearly represents a departure from conventional practice, which makes information gathering independent of formal judgements. Not only are these opportunities purposeful for the designer in challenging conventional thinking, but they are useful for the client, who becomes sensitized to the implications of form and meaning in the early stages of the design process (Sanoff,1984).

Many of the programming models are characterized by a predominantly client-centered turnkey approach, in which the architect's responsibility ceases with the completion of the building. Because clients are not often users, and because buildings undergo considerable growth and change during their lifetime, the programming process needs to take these factors into account.

Although most practitioners have stressed the importance of client participation, direct involvement of the user has been given insufficient attention because it raises a number of methodological questions. Issues such as who should get involved are as crucial as the client's willingness to act on employees' reactions to the environment. These concerns address the core of facility programming, and the architect's role in the process.

Not only questions of user satisfaction are important; so are satisfaction and management policies affecting the use of the environment. Perhaps the most important facet of facility programming is the knowledge that existing or analogous situations are a major source of input into subsequent design phases. Learning about different ways in which the environment is used is an effective tool for gathering information, and developing helpful insights into a building's performance.

Linking data collection to programming

Effective programming depends on knowing what types of data are needed, and on selecting the appropriate means of obtaining and documenting them. There are a variety of techniques for obtaining information directly from the source (Michelson, 1975; Sanoff, 1978; Zeisel,1981; see especially Marans & Ahrentzen, 1987, and Low, 1987), of which walk-throughs are one. User reports through surveys and questionnaires are used for collecting opinions and attitudes, and observation methods, data logs, and standardized forms seek descriptive information. Both descriptive and evaluative data can be applied at various stages in the programming process. Background information from other than user reports is equally necessary and can be derived from analyzing existing data, literature, and records (Jones, 1970), as well as from programmers' observations and insights.

A unique approach to health-care-facility programming is used by Stone, Marrachini, and Patterson (Tusler, Schraishuhn, & Meyer, 1985), who described two different user groups: patients (the primary users of health-care

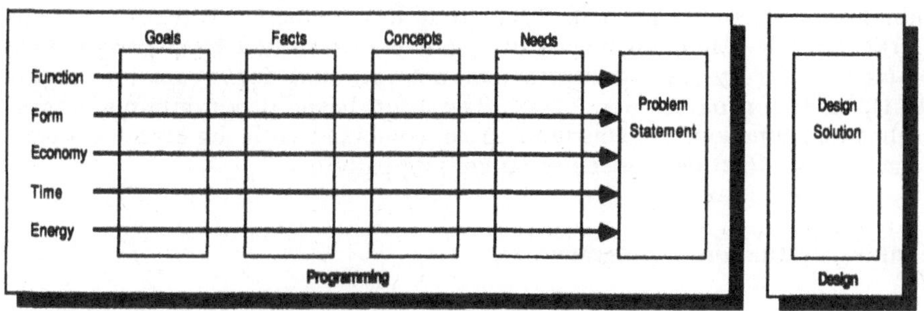

Figure 1.6 Pena's programming process

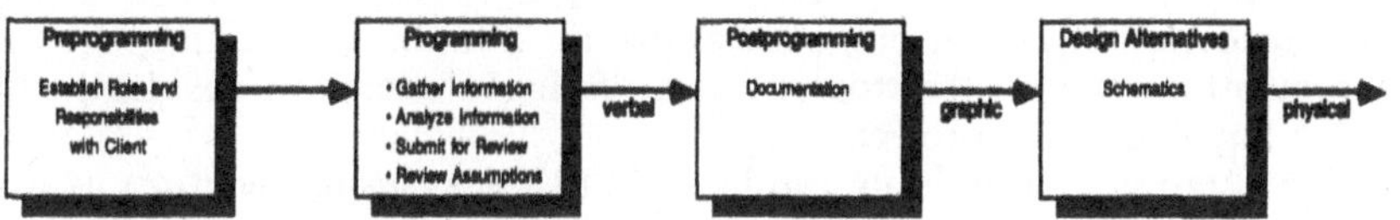

Figure 1.7 White's programming process

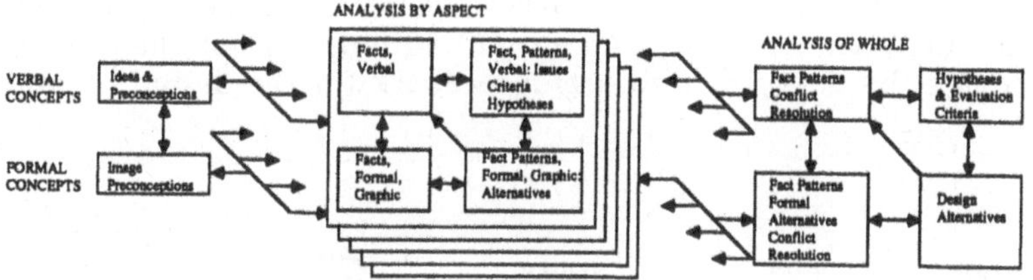

Figure 1.9 Robinson and Weeks' process: Interaction between programming and design

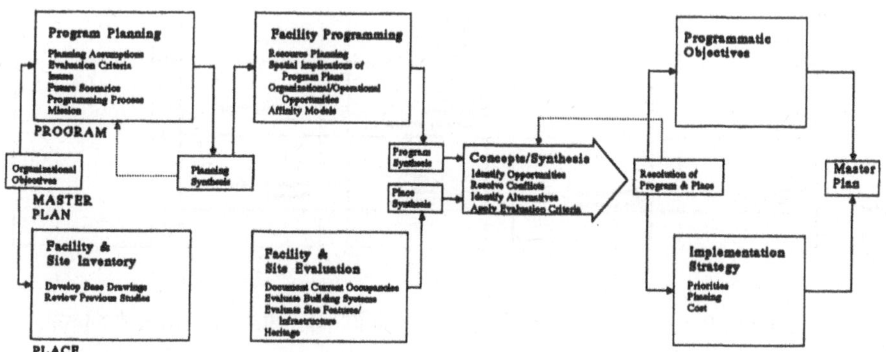

Figure 1.10 Master-plan integrated process. (Hellmuth, Obata, & Kassabaum, 1990.)

facilities) and the service providers, including nurses, physicians, administrators, and technicians. Each group has unique needs that relate to its particular role. Matching needs to resources, illustrated by a pattern or a framework for organizing information, analysis, and documentation (Figure 1.11), is the programmer's task. The four basic programming stages-utilization, function, systems, and space, combined with the areas of study-form a matrix that defines the programming pattern.

Linking evaluation to programming

Environmental assessment, or the post-occupancy evaluation (POE) is the practice of using methods such as surveys, questionnaires, and observation's of people's behavior to discover exactly what makes the designed environment work well for its users. POEs are a procedure that involves the user in their own assessment of their everyday physical environment. POEs can be effective in correcting environmental errors by examining buildings in use, or in preventing potential errors by use of the information results in the programming stages of a project.

An evaluation of a building can be used to assess design features as well as the program. Frequently, a POE traces a building malfunction to a false assumption in the programming process. Evaluations have also helped to convince clients to choose design alternatives that they might not otherwise have considered. Some architectural firms carry out their own evaluations in order to measure building performance against the original program, to acquaint the designer with the opinions and attitudes of the client or user, and to provide the designer with useful feedback for the design of similar facilities.

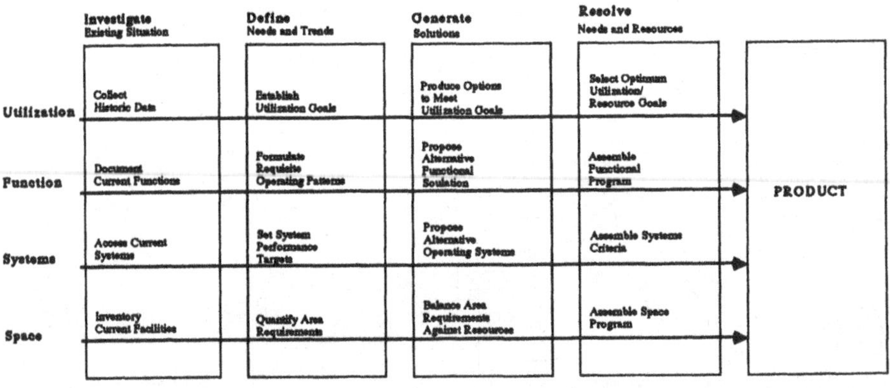

Figure 1.11 Programming pattern overview (Tusler, Schraishuhn & Meyer)

One of the world's largest building clients, the U.S. General Services Administration (GSA, has routinely performed comprehensive post-occupancy evaluations since 1976 (Zimring & Reizenstein, 1981). These evaluations use teams that include an architect, a mechanical engineer, an electrical engineer, and a psychologist. Because the evaluations cover a broad range of issues, including behavior, energy,and cost-effectiveness, the most significant results of this process have been the way in which the GSA works with architects. Because the evaluation process compares the program with the completed building, the evaluations have helped in the development of a more straightforward programming process, one with which both architects and clients are more pleased.

Recognizing that agencies providing large numbers of housing units need to assess their own products in order to better fulfill resident's needs, The Greater London Council (GLC) developed a system of housing appraisal surveys. The purpose of the procedure was to assess GLC tenents' opinions of the built environment outside and inside the building. The information collected is used to improve the programming and design of future housing projects. This information is complemented by observations made by GLC staff who survey the selected housing projects. The social survey method used for the Program of Housing Surveys is the Housing Appraisal Kit, which was developed jointly by the GLC and the Department of the Environment.

New Zealand's Ministry of Works and Development (MWD) and Victoria University at Wellington's School of Architecture (VUW) undertook a multiyear project to develop methods for the post-occupancy evaluation of government buildings (Daish, Gray, Kernohan, & Salmond, 1982). The MWD believed that an effective POE process could improve the quality of information, communication, and decision making in its building delivery activities, and could thus enhance the quality of the program and the building. Central to the success of their POEs was the development of an appropriate process for gathering information. One method of evaluation used is described as a 'walk-through' (see Gray, Watson, Daish, & Kernohan, 1985). This is a common method, often found in practice, of evaluating a building's performance by walking through and noting its salient features. The process involves two sets of people with distinct roles: a number of participant groups, and one Task Group. The role of the members of the participant group is to evaluate the building from this group's point of view. Its members are drawn from among those with an interest in the occupied building. The role of the task group, which consists of the VUW research team, is to help the participant group in making evaluations. The task group plans and manages the evaluation tasks, records and evaluates the data, and writes the subsequent review. In planning for evaluation, a number of walk-throughs are scheduled, each with a small group of participants representing a particular interest in the building or project. Each walk-through involves the participant group and the task group in three connected activities: introductory meeting, a touring interview, and a review meeting. Following the walk-through, the participants and the task group meet to review the comments made during the walk-through, and to form recommendations concerning the building and its functioning. When all walk-throughs are completed, the task group transcribes and classifies the participant groups' recommendation for reference and action.

Programming for Digital Equipment Corporation: A case study

The objective of this project was to develop space planning standards for Digital Equipment Corporation (DEC), an international computer company. A branch office located in North Carolina, a major sales district within the national organization, served as the site for this project. The firm of The Adams Group, Architects, was selected to develop a new approach towards space planning that would improve employee's work environments and lower facility operating costs, as well as incorporate user perceptions and preferences for new office settings.

In anticipation of future changes, namely an office move, the DEC District office formed a twelve member Task group composed of managers, professionals, clerical, and support staff to investigate an approach for improving office quality and productivity, while reducing operating expenses. All group members were encouraged to participate in open discussions, and communicate individual concerns and opinions. The Task group believed that an open decision making process, involving a variety of user groups, would produce design guidelines that would resolve the employee dissatisfaction associated with their current space planning standards.

Since the aim of this project was to develop a new approach to space planning, the process initiated by the programming team began with the identification of project goals. To facilitate this activity, the Nominal Group Technique (NGT), a goal setting strategy, was used (Delbecq, van de Ven, & Gustafson,1975). In this approach, goals were identified by participants and recorded on index cards. Participants then discussed their ideas which were recorded on a large sheet of brown paper. All the goal statements were rewritten to eliminate redundancy and prioritized. The following statements represent the collective view of the Task group:

- Provide an office environment that satisfies employees' personal office needs.
- Develop an office environment which best supports DEC's image as an innovator in office systems.
- Provide many opportunities for DEC employees to participate in the development of design guidelines. The product must be creative in PROCESS and PRODUCT.
- Create opportunities for achieving significant operating cost reductions.
- Improve office interior quality, including light, color, furniture, and shared areas, such as libraries and break areas.

Task group members were also asked to generate ideas about the 'office of the future.'The technique used to enable participants to fantasize about the future was a Wish Poem: a series of statements preceded by the phrase 'I wish my office...' This approach alllows a free flow of ideas and feelings. The following statements are representative of the groups feelings:

An earlier version of this article appeared in *Design Studies*, 9, 1 (1988): 14-24.

I wish my office would incorporate lighting that creates a natural effect
I wish my office was accessible to windows, skylights, and open space
I wish my office would create a positive professional impression on employees and visitors
I wish my office had exercise/shower facilities
I wish my office had a nice cafeteria
I wish my office would allow needed privacy at times
I wish my office would incorporate furniture,work space, and storage that is appropriate for computer office automation
I wish my office would create a feeling that I am working for a company that cares about my well-being and consequently the productivity of its employees while they are at work
I wish my office would not necessarily look like an office

In order to assess the performance of the present office areas, and gain an understanding of the functions of DEC, a space inventory was conducted where information based on activity units was recorded (Figure 1.12). Specific data was recorded on user privacy, floor area, occupancy time, and shared space. One of the issues that emerged was that DEC assigned floor area, furnishings, and equipment based on the their organizational structure, rather than on the performance requirements of the users. This corporate design tendency often produces problems of misfit between functional requirements and corporate standards (Brill & BOSTI, 1984).

To further substantiate these issues, and gain an understanding of employee attitudes about their office environment, a 50 item questionnaire was administered to over one-half of the employees. The office survey was intended to identify exisiting conflicts for DEC employees, their relationship to current planning criteria, and attitudes towards their present work environment. The questions were divided into three major categories:

- those causing physical health hazards
- those affecting people's relationships to each other, and to their work environment
- those that impede the work effectiveness of individuals and groups.

In addition, an environmental reaction scale was included in the questionnaire to assess employee's reactions to the 'sufficiency' of their work place. On a three point scale, 15 characteristics were listed for employee's to rate their present work place, as well as to rate the sufficency of those character- stics. For example, employee's describe their work environment as 'some- what adaptable,' but 'not adaptable enough.'

Respondents also indicated that existing office areas are too small, and the open office plan results in a large amount of unusable floor space. Privacy, both visual and acoustic, in the open office was also described as an area of dissatisfaction. While glare was reported to be a problem, the highest level of agreement confirmed the desire for windows in all work areas.

This accumulated knowledge and experience was recorded on Activity Unit Summary Sheets (Figure 1.13). These Summary Sheets provided the basic documentation necessary for future discussions, review sessions, and workshops.

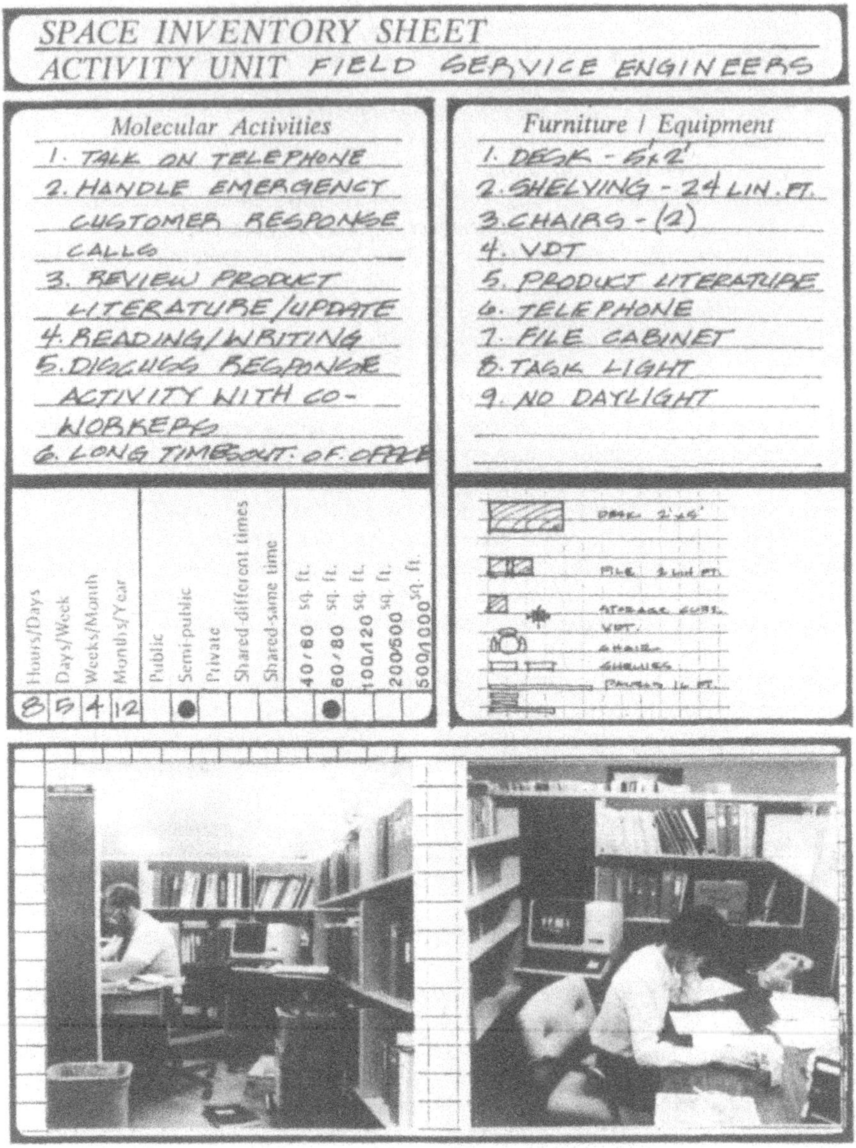

SPACE INVENTORY SHEET

ACTIVITY UNIT FIELD SERVICE ENGINEERS

Molecular Activities
1. TALK ON TELEPHONE
2. HANDLE EMERGENCY CUSTOMER RESPONSE CALLS
3. REVIEW PRODUCT LITERATURE/UPDATE
4. READING/WRITING
5. DISCUSS RESPONSE ACTIVITY WITH CO-WORKERS
6. LONG TIMES OUT OF OFFICE

Furniture / Equipment
1. DESK - 5'x2'
2. SHELVING - 24 LIN. FT.
3. CHAIRS - (2)
4. VDT
5. PRODUCT LITERATURE
6. TELEPHONE
7. FILE CABINET
8. TASK LIGHT
9. NO DAYLIGHT

Hours/Days	Days/Week	Weeks/Month	Months/Year	Public	Semi-public	Private	Shared-different times	Shared-same time	40/60 sq. ft.	60/80 sq. ft.	100/120 sq. ft.	200/500 sq. ft.	500/1000 sq. ft.
8	5	4	12		●					●			

Figure 1.12 Space inventory sheet example

PRIMARY ACTIVITY UNIT SUMMARY SHEET

ACTIVITY UNIT

Molecular Activities

1. Talk On Telephone
2. Review New Equipment
3. Enter New Sales
4. Review New Sales Techniques
5. Discuss Sales Activity With Manager
6. Reading/ Writing
7. File New Manual Data

Hours/Days	Days/Week	Weeks/Month	Months/Year	Public	Semi-public	Private	Shared-different times	Shared-same time	40/60 sq. ft.	60/80 sq. ft.	100/120 sq. ft.	200/500 sq. ft.	500/1000 sq. ft.
2	2	4	12		●		●			●			

Furniture & Equipment

1. Work Surface For Writing – 9 Lin. Ft.
2. Layout Area For Books/ Manuals
3. Access To VDT
4. Shelving For Product Guides – 6'
5. Comfortable Chair
6. Access To Files

Environmental Requirements

1. Task Lighting For Work Surface
2. Low Direct Light For VDT/ Reduce Contrasts
3. Indirect Ambient Area Lighting

Floorspace Requirements

80 sq. ft.

- Privacy Control
- Shelving/ Product Manuals
- Personal Storage
- File Storage
- Work Surface
- Personal Items Drawer
- Task Light
- Comfortable Chair
- Layoff Area
- VDT Area
- Background Control

9'

8'

Figure 1.13 Program sheet sample

An important step in the development of the program was a workshop consisting of the Task group and representatives of each department and functional area. The twenty-two participants who volunteered were divided into three workgroups, where they discussed office objectives and compared them to specific design alternatives. Spatial objectives generated in earlier meetings were circulated to all groups. They included such statements as:

- provide views to outside windows
- utilize space more efficiently
- increase opportunity for interpersonal communication.

This list, in conjunction with the data sheets, served as a basis for collective group discussions about the functional areas, and their requirements. Once the purposes of the office had been identified, and appropriate functions discussed, participants were prepared to develop a plan for their ideal office. To facilitate this stage of the process, a 1/4 inch scale model of a typical office floor was provided with a floor grid, partitions, and a variety of storage components. Since it was anticipated that many options might be discussed, floor plans of the model were made available for sketching purposes. Work groups discussed issues, made trade-offs, compared ideas, and selected the best option. The objectives for the preferred option were as follows:

- Develop neighborhood zones for each functional area to increase departmental identity.
- Provide views to perimeter window areas.
- Reduce through traffic within functional areas.
- Increase the opportunity for interpersonal communication.
- Improve quality of break areas.
- Develop libraries for reference material that provide alternative places to work.
- Utilize space more efficiently by developing shared work stations.
- Provide better working relationships between department's managers and support staff.
- Increase the number of private conference areas.
- Provide an open plan layout that will provide flexibility. Only 'manager's of people' should have private offices.

This option was based on a concept where activity areas would be consolidated to allow for a shared work station for sales/field service engineers who are often out of the office. Manager's private offices were internally located which permitted window areas to remain open. Several conference areas were proposed for small group meetings for those occasions requiring privacy. Common activity areas, such as the library, were proposed as reference areas, and additional work space.

The workshop was instrumental since it allowed unique concepts, such as the shared work station to emerge from the participants, an idea that might not have been considered when utilizing more traditional design methods. Approximately 60 people throughout the DEC office reviewed the various team recommendations, as well as participants sharing their ideas with each other.

A computer simulation of the workshop results allowed the Task group to visualize how the office environment would appear. The interactive CAD system utilized, permitted continuous modifications and refinements as a variety of needs were discussed. The proposed office environment represents an increase in the amount of work surface, and a more open work area. This design solution responded to employees desire to encourage greater eye contact, and the potential for increased interpersonal communication, more so than the existing office 'cubes' provide (Figure 1.15 & 1.16). Several types of shared work areas, or Touchdown Station's, were designed to accommodate specific tasks for sales representatives and field service engineers. The Touchdown Station allowed DEC to achieve the goal of reducing operating costs resulting from a reduction of almost 50% of floor area.

Participants also agreed to the planning concept of 'neighborhoods' within each department. This was viewed as a method of reducing noise and traffic problems identified from the office survey.The transition zones located between neighborhoods are shared activity areas, such as libraries, and break rooms (Figure 1.14). The acceptance of new office planning guidelines was a direct outgrowth of the open process which encouraged involvement of the DEC employees. They consequently became a standard for the district office.

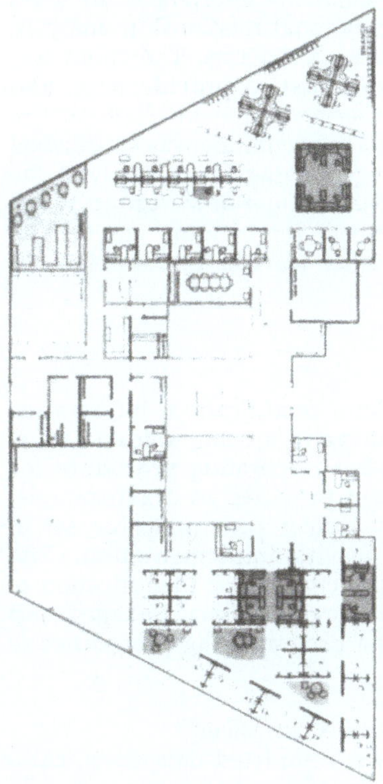

Figure 1.14 Floor plan of branch office

Figure 1.15 CAD simulation of office interior (before)

Figure 1.16 CAD simulation of office interior (after)

Programming a research facility: A case study

The results of this study of user needs were intended to provide the initial information for a more complete program for a new engineering research building. The 44,ooo sq. ft facility, to be located on the campus of a multi-disciplinary research complex in North Carolina, was to house a variety of research operations which relied heavily on computer applications. The objectives of the programming process, conducted by N. C. State University's, Community Development Group (Sanoff, 1981), were to identify activities and activity relationships, and user perceptions of, and preferences for office settings. A variety of data collection and analysis techniques were employed by the programming team, including standardized programming sheets, relationship matrices, correlation diagrams, and questionnaires containing verbal rating scales and open ended questions. The program represented the user-related space requirements for the building, and was intended as a guide for the architect, and a model for the client in continuing development of program information.

The objective of the project was to develop a program of space requirements for a specialized facility based on individual and group activities, and user preferences. The project involved three elements interrelated to space needs: activity analysis, functional and organizational relationship analysis, and evaluation of perceived adequacy of office workplaces. The client was actively involved in the programming process; first to provide data, and second, to gain a clear understanding of the user-environment relationships, their perceptions, and their needs. A facility study committee was established by the client to project space needs. The programming team involved the management and research staff, through individual interviews, group workshops, and questionnaires. Forty-one staff members, representing three levels of organizational position, participated in the office workplace evaluation.

Process

Programming, in part, is a process of problem identification, information collection, and information organization resulting in a communicable statement of intent (Sanoff, 1977). Programming is an operating procedure for systematizing the design process. The program provides an organizational structure for the design of the facility, and a clear communicable set of conditions fro review by those affected by its implementation. The development of the program included three principal tasks: identification of user activities, identification of functional and organizational linkages, and evaluation of the workplace. An outline of the programming procedures is presented below:

1. Programmer devised standardized data collection sheet.
2. Department managers, during interviews, completed data sheet, cataloging activites, personal, space, and equipment and storage needs.
3. Programmer compared secondary activities (those necessary to accomplish primary activites) with each other in a relationship diagram for each divison or department.

4. Activities were grouped from matrix into correlation diagrams of principal functions within each division or department.
5. Programmer prepared department/division/function interaction matrix for use in interviews with department managers.
6. Department managers identified relationships by matrix among functions/divisions/departments.
7. Programmer mapped relationship patterns from matrix in an interaction net.
8. Programmer administered 'perception survey' to obtain user evaluations of office environments.
9. Programmer analyzed results of survey.
10. Programmer documented findings and presented program to designer and client.

An activity analysis was performed to enable the programmer, and ultimately the client and architect, to understand the nature of the facility functions and their relationships. The initial step entailed the preparation of a programming data sheet which was used by all departments to collect and record information pertaining to their activities and needs (Figure 1.17).

In interviews with department managers, the programming sheets were filled out, identifying organizational elements (division/department), primary activities, participants (personnel), space requirements for those activities (size, support requirements, level of privacy needed), the secondary activities necessary to necessary to accomplish the primary activities, and the equipment/storage needs.

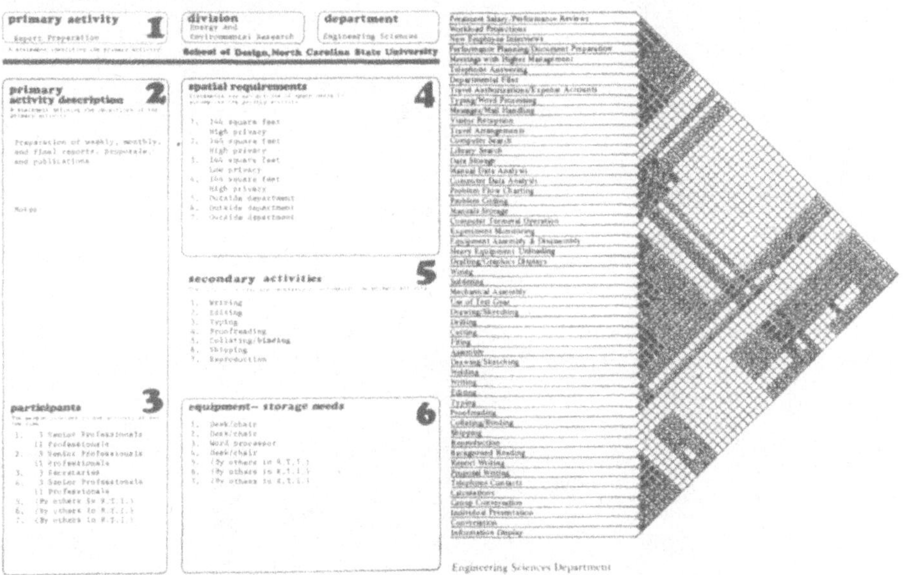

Figure 1.17 Program data sheet

Figure 1.18 Activity matrix showing proximity relationships

When all the programming sheets were completed, the secondary activities of each division or department were listed in a relationship (or affinity) matrix. This was used to identify the proximity relationships of the activities performed by comparing each activity to each other one. Three criteria were considered in completing the matrix: did the activity occur in the same space as another activity, in close proximity to it, or independent of the other activity. The proximity relationships of activities are shown in Figure 1.18.

From the matrix it was possible for the programmer to identify groups of activities that occurred within the same space, and the activity groupings that related to each other. To clarify these functional-space relationships, the programmer developed a correlation diagram identifying the specialized function spaces, and their connections to each other. In Figure 1.19, for example, the activities of the secretarial function occur within the same physical area and have a functional relationship with the activities occuring in the department office, and the conference area.

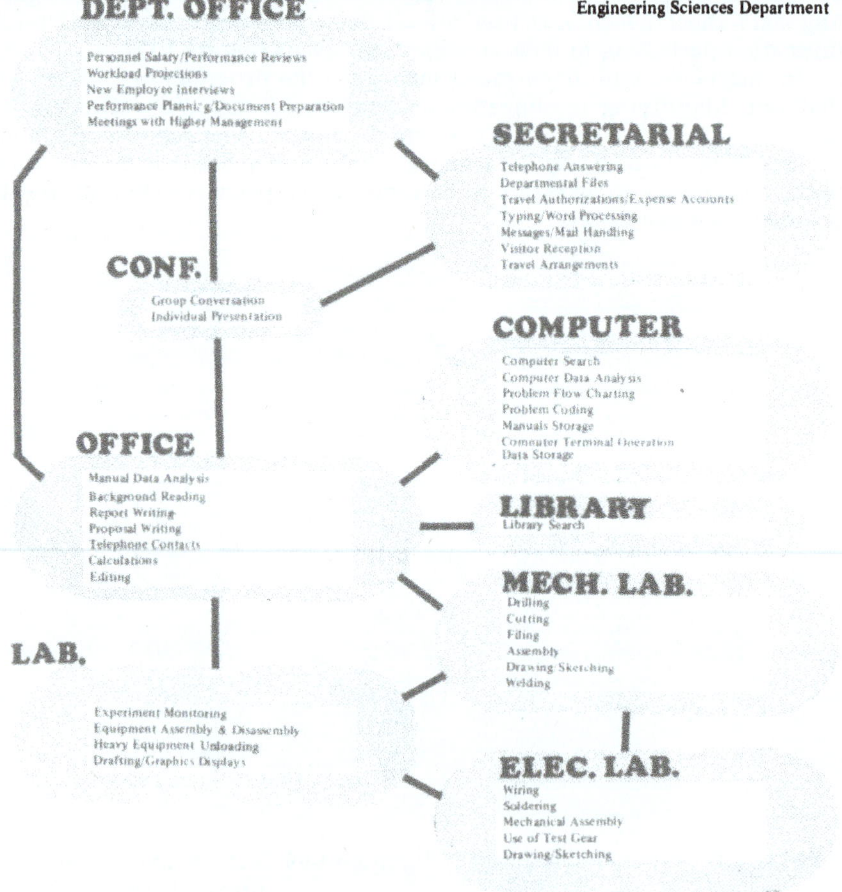

Figure 1.19 Functional relationships

Since the activities of any one department within the engineering research group are often connected with the activities of other departments, the programmer then turned to identifying those relationships. Another matrix, listing each departemnt and its divisions and functions was created and the department managers were asked to identify the working relationships with other departments by their indication on a diagram.

When the interviews and diagrams were completed, a composite matrix was created and conflicting information was resolved in review sessions with managers (Figure 1.20). The results were further clarified by drawing an interaction net diagram. Departments with a higher degree of interaction were grouped together, and less frequent interactions were identified by connecting lines.

Energy and Environmental Research Division	**Process Engineering**
	Engineering Sciences
	Geosciences
	Economics
Systems and Measurements Division	**Systems Instruementation**
	Environmental Measurements
	Systems Engineering
Operations Analysis Division	**Management Information Sciences**
	Applied Ecology
	Applications Programming
Technology Applications Center	**Biomedical Engineering**
	Technology and Resource Management

Figure 1.20 Composite matrix of departmental relationships

The final step in the programming process consisted of a workplace assessment survey. Here participants rated their present offiice and four photographs of different offices, using a verbal scale of opposite descriptors (Figure 1.21). The results of the assessment provided a basis for a series of follow-up, open-ended questions using the same photographs (Figure 1.22). They were as follows:

- What aspects of their present office they liked.
- Their preferences for the 'ideal' office.
- The reasons for their ratings in the visual assessment scale.

When commenting on characteristics of their present office, most respondents felt indifferent to their workplace. There were often expressions of discomfort in windowless offices, while those sharing offices complained about the lack of privacy. Dissenting comments about office appearance and comfort were numerous and wide ranging, such as 'drab colors' and institutional (Figure 1.23). Reactions to the photographed offices were rich in detail, especially with reference to appearance and image. where respondents projected themselves into each setting as they considered advantages and disadvantages. In general, most facility users preferred the 'closed' to the 'open' offices, depicted in the photographs.

The involvement of the client, and the users in the programming process was intended to sensitize them to their own behavior, their working environments, and the interrelationships between them. This was important since the results of previous experience with poorly designed facilities left the users with low expectations of future possibilities. Since previous discussions with facility users revealed the impact of the physical environment on productivity and job satisfaction, the client and the architect, Clark, Tribble, Harris and Li, supported the development for a high quality building. User preferences for private offices separated from the laboratory influenced CTH&L's decision to design closed offices with a view, privacy, and natural light for all staff (Figure 1.22).

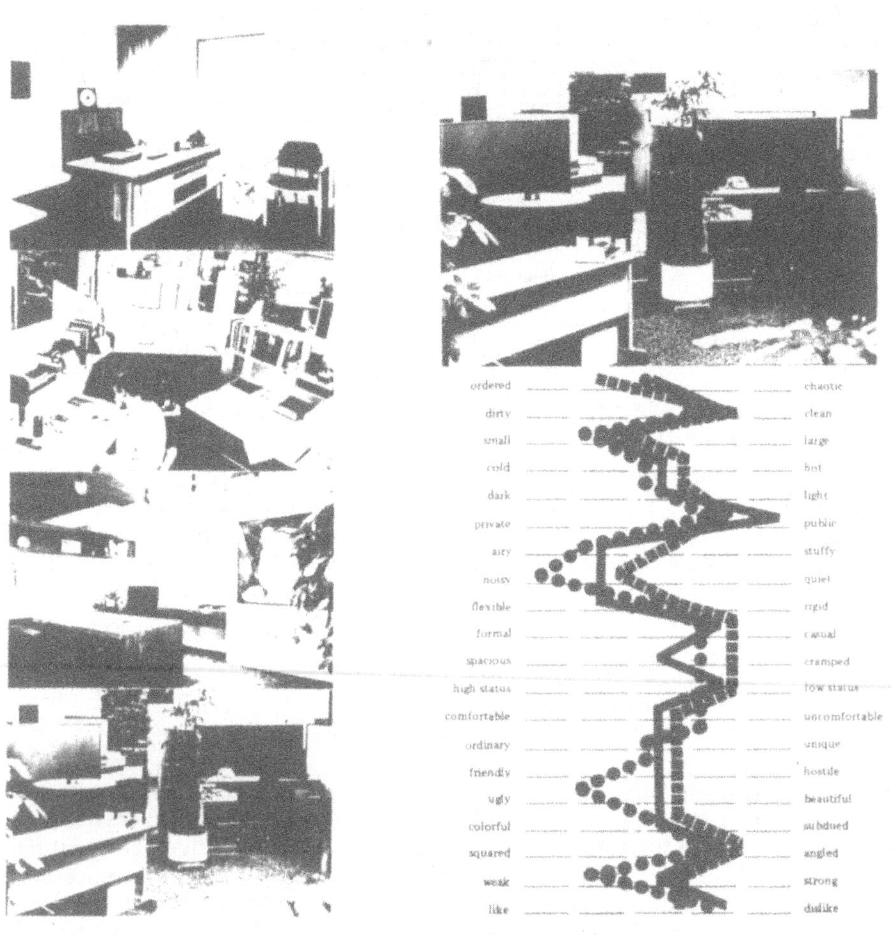

Figure 1.21 Visual assessment scale

Discussions with office workers prior to the move indicated that the central clerical pool was poorly located to suport the professional staff, and inadequately illuminated. Recognizing this, CTH&L rearranged the clerical pool into groups adjacent to staff offices where they were provided with ample daylight (Figure 1.23); a striking difference from their previous office.

Involvement in the programming process raised the awareness of the client/user to the impact of the physical environment on their performance. CTH&L reported this as a major contributing factor to produce an effective building, since they understood the user's concerns and expectations.

Acknowledgment

The first version of this article was written by H. Sanoff, G.Adams, & A. Smith, and published in Palmer, M. (ed.), 1981, *The Architect's Guide to Facility Programming,* American Institute of Architects, Washington, DC. Another version was published in *Design Studies*, 6,4 (1988): 187-195.

Figure 1.22 Photographs showing perimeter offices and daylight in secretarial areas

Figure 1.23 Photographs of existing offices

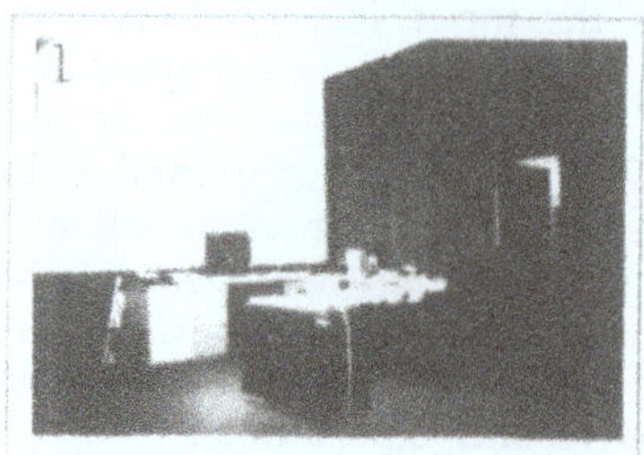

Office Evaluation Questionnaire

List the picture numbers in rank order according to the image you have of an ideal office space.

SAMPLE

Choose one adjective form each pair to describe each of the five pictures. Circle the picture number to show your choice.

1 2 3 4 5	Cheerful	Gloomy	1 2 3 4 5
1 2 3 4 5	Comfortable	Uncomfortable	1 2 3 4 5
1 2 3 4 5	Dark	Light	1 2 3 4 5
1 2 3 4 5	Imaginative	Unimaginative	1 2 3 4 5
1 2 3 4 5	Inviting	Repelling	1 2 3 4 5
1 2 3 4 5	Noisy	Quiet	1 2 3 4 5
1 2 3 4 5	Spacious	Cramped	1 2 3 4 5
1 2 3 4 5	Variety	Monotony	1 2 3 4 5

2 Evaluation

Evaluation research is an area of activity devoted to collecting, analyzing, and interpreting information on the need, implementation, and impact of any intervention (social program or environmental impact) efforts to better the lot of humankind, and to improve social conditions and community life.

The commitment of various professions to systematically evaluate programs in such fields as education, and public health goes back to the turn of the twentieth century. The concerns at that time were to provide literacy and occupational training by the most effective and economical means and to reduce the mortality of infectious diseases.

By the 1950's, large scale evaluation programs were commonplace. Evaluations of delinquency prevention programs, penal-rehabilitation projects, public housing programs, and community organization activities were being undertaken in in the U.S. and Europe. Social surveys and computer assisted statistical analysis became widespread. By the late 1960's, evaluation research had become a 'growth industry.' During the 1970's, a variety of books were published, including texts, books of readings, a magazine entitled *Evaluation,* and the *Evaluation Quarterly*.

Design evaluation research

Environmental design evaluation is an outgrowth of this recent development, and is based on the belief that the professions can learn from both its accomplishments and mistakes. Evaluation can provide feedback to clients and designers on the impact of the physical environment on people's behavior. Immediate feedback enables the ease of improvements while, without it, change is difficult. Based on the belief that architectural journalism can use a new dimension, Donald Canty (1974), editor of *Architecture,* the Journal of the American Instiute of Architects, stated that,'today the American architectural scene is filled with buildings that don't work, laboratories that hinder research, university buildings that disregard student and faculty needs alike, and libraries that satisfy the custodial staff, but ignore the needs of users and librarians. One might conclude that some architects don't care about satisfying human needs, or they lack the human know how to design for people.'

Design evaluation is concerned with assessing the effectiveness of designed environments for users. There are, however, two schools of thought that have emerged, drawing their methods from the social and behavioral sciences. They can be described as attitudinal evaluation and behavioral evaluation. Both approaches stem from the concern for validity or the extent to which a particular technique appears to measure what it claims to measure. Other validity concerns are related to the extent of which evaluation data can be used to estimate activities in an environment in certain, current, or future situations.

Craik (1968) compared the assessment of personality and the assessment of environments, and suggested the use of approaches developed by personality researchers such as free association, adjective check-lists, questionnaires, and so on. Clearly, each technique requires an imposition on the individual in terms of time, energy, and willingness to cooperate.

Canter (1970) disinguishes between studying building users as 'subjects,' and as 'objects.' This distinction is related to our assumption about the factors responsible for a person's behavior. Some assume that behavior can be attributed to external circumstances that 'push' the individual in various directions. A view of people as 'objects' tends to focus the evaluation on observing people's behavior as a basis for drawing inferences and reasons for the behavior. Those who see users as 'subjects,' such as Craik, prefer to hear what people have to say about their environmental preferences and actions.

The position advanced here is that a more comprehensive understanding of people and the environment can best be understood by employing a number of techniques that involve the user as a subject as well as an object.

In a mammoth 3 1/2 year study of 37 housing developments throughout the U.S., resident satisfaction was the focus for the evaluation. The reasons for this point of view was due to the apparent undesirable social and operational consequences of ignoring residents' attitudes as well as the limited resident's input into housing research, or the formulation and evaluation of housing policy.

Although there have been numerous housing research studies, they generally tend to stress one aspect such as building type preferences (Canter & Thorne, 1976), or the issue of crime prevention through design (Newman, 1973). The research team led by Francescato (1980) examined the interdependence of all factors, and explain residents satisfaction as the influence of three aspects. In order of importance, these are 'satisfaction with other residents, 'pleasant appearance' of units, buildings, and grounds, and the development as a whole, and the'perceived economic value' represented by living in the development. Each of these aspects are interrelated with each other and are explained by conditions of having friendly and helpful neighbors, and management rules, and a sense of having control over one's life. Cooper-

Marcus and Sarkissian (1986) collected approximately one hundred housing evaluation case studies as the basis of their book, *Housing as if People Mattered*. Their intent was to use the results of POE research to generate design guidelines.

The issue of environmental appearance is also one of considerable speculative research. Ruesch and Kees (1956), in their book, *Non-Verbal Communication*, point to clues imbedded in buildings and landscapes that have something to say about the status, prestige, and other values of those who own them. Krampen (1979) believes in his research in Semiology, or the science of meaning, where the environment is transmitting messages as a means of influencing people to do something or letting them know something. Rainwater (1956) describes the following message with respect to public housing:

> *The physical evidence of trash, poor plumbing, and the stink that goes with it, rats and other vermin, deepen their feelings for being moral outcasts. Their physical world is telling them that they are inferior and bad just as effectively perhaps as do their human interactions.*

Bettelheim (1974) has written of the importance of what he calls 'silent messages,' which convey an institutions intentions through the minute details of the physical environment. The appearance of a building, then, is an environmental message. By improving the appearance of their individual units, a family living in a public housing can proclaim its individuality and counteract a negative message that the building itself conveys about the residents. Oscar Newman (1973) found that increased security seemed to result in increased personalization of interior spaces. Since increased security was attributed to a clear definition of exterior spaces, and evidence of maintenance and personalization of semiprivate outdoor areas, it is evident that the visibility of community pride among the residents helped to improve relationships between them. This is significant since evaluation studies have shown that residents of many high density housing projects perceive themselves as respectable, but their neighbors as 'unsavory characters.'

Observation, can also be used to better understand people's behavior in the environment. Psychologist, Proshansky (1965) observed and recorded the activities of patients in hospital rooms. Comparing the sociability of patients in single rooms, double rooms, and wards, they found that when the number of patients in a room is smaller, social activity is greater. Willems (1972) observed the locations of patients activities in a hospital, and found that the area of patients' activity is small in comparison with the total hospital size.

Evaluation research, generally referred to as post-occupancy evaluation (POE), is a form of professional accountability that seeks to improve the art, as well as the science of architecture. The process of evaluation is the missing link between implementation and future programming in the staging of building design operations.

Post-occupancy evaluation process

A POE can be applied to any type or size of environment or facility. The type of POE utilized for a particular situation is a function of the amount of time available, the resources, and the depth of knowledge necessary. Preiser, Rabinowitz, and White (1988) describes three distinct levels in carrying out a POE-*indicative, investigative, and diagnostic-* each consisting of the phases of planning, conducting, and applying the POE.

An indicative POE is a short term process that seeks to identify major successes and failures. The methods of collecting information consist of questionnaires, walk-throughs, and interviews usually conducted with a committee representing the client's organization. Questions ordinarily focus on issues related to performance, spatial adequacy, and image. A walk-through assessment of the entire facility relies on direct observation to verify issues that may have emerged from the questionnaire. Interviews, and a summary of findings conclude the the process.

An investigative POE, according to Preiser et al., (1988), is a more extensive investigation that relies on a literature search to establish evaluative criteria, as well as comparisons with analogous situations. The phases of the investigative POE are identical to those of the indicative POE.

The most detailed and comprehensive approach is the diagnostic POE, where many data collection methods are used, including questionnaires, surveys, observations, and physical measurements (Preiser et al., 1988). These studies are long-term in nature, and tend to focus on a building type, rather than a particular facility.

Prior to initiating a POE, there are several preliminary steps that require consideration, in preparation for on-site data collection. Client briefing about the nature of the process, the type of activities involved, and shared responsibilities are necessary before conducting the POE. This would be the stage where research methods and analytical techniques would be determined (Preiser et al., 1988). In addition, background information, such as building documentation, client's organizational structure, and liason individuals, is necessary to establish a POE plan. The plan will include the development of specific information gathering methods, sampling methods, authorization for photographs and surveys, and data recording sheets. Initially, observing the building under working conditions for several hours will be sufficient to prepare a data collection plan.

The primary tasks in conducting the POE are the collection and analysis of data. Timing, too, is important in order to minimize disruption of functions in the client organization. Therefore, coordination with the building occupants will facilitate the distribution and collection of data-recording forms, and other printed materials necessary for a manageable evaluation process.

Data collection and analysis precedes the interpretation of the results into useful findings. Reporting and presenting the findings of the POE are integral to the client's understanding of the results. POE findings typically describe, interpret, and explain the performance of a building (Presier et al., 1988). After extensive discussion of the findings, recommendations for future action takes place.

Evaluation methods

There are a variety of methods by which we can learn about the physical environment. Appraisal measures the interaction between the human observer and the physical environment. This section includes a representative array of methods for eliciting user information that can substantially aid the designer in decision making. Studies of the environment involve four groups of variables (Craik, 1968): observers, modes of observation, environments, and attributes of the environment. Each of the methods can be used to answer a variety of evaluation questions.

- Observation and behavioral mapping is a way to look at what people do in the physical environment.
- Social mapping helps to explore and identify relationships between people in the physical environment.
- Adjective rating scales are used to obtain an impression of a group's reaction to some aspect of the physical environment.

Observation and behavioral mapping

Observation can be used to better understand people's behavior in the environment. It is a method of looking at action between people and their environment.The word *environment* might here include everything except the people themselves; the environment can be an entire building, a part of a building, or an outdoor area.

People may modify their actions, however, if they realize they are being observed. Observing unobtrusively allows the study of people's behavior without their realizing that their activities are important. In crowded areas or busy streets, observers may go unnoticed. In some environments, observers may take part in the activities, while in others it may be necessary for observers to position themselves in remote locations. Valuable information can be obtained when behavior is systematically recorded. Casual observation may result in incomplete findings that show only what seems to be obvious. Carefully planned observation will enable designers to accurately collect and use the information that describes human behavior. In order to observe systematically, the following components should be considered (Sanoff, 1981).

- What might one need to know about people? Important information could include the number of persons, the amount of time each is observed, the sex, age, and location of each person, and whether people are in groups. A data sheet can be constructed to record such information (Figure 2.1 & 2.2). The observer can also record whether a person's behavior is active or passive. Active behavior is when participation is necessary for an activity to continue, and passive if the activity would continue without that participation.
- Activities will be the thing people are doing-the defined physical interaction between a person and an environmental feature or cue. Having been designed to support specific activities, environmental cues convey silent messages to people about what activities should occur in a space.

Time of Day
Date
Day of Week
Weather

MAIN FLOOR	Walking		Social Behavior		Other Activities		Total	
	E	O	E	O	E	O	E	O
Entrance lobby								
Major lounge								
Library								
Craft room								
Mailbox area								
Elevator area								
Total								

FLOOR	Open Doors	Laundry	Lounge		Hallway		Total	
			E	O	E	O	E	O
2								
3								
4								
5								
6								
7								
8								
9								
10								
11								
12								
13								
14								
Total								

Figure 2.1 Behavior settings data sheet used to organize and record information about people

GENERAL INFORMATION

Location of Observer
Time of Observation
Date
Weather Conditions

Activity Types
Objects Used
Physical Parts

PARTICIPANT INVENTORY

Participant	Black Male	Black Female	White Male	White Female
Infant				
Preschool				
Young Ch.				
Adolescent				
Teenager				
Adult				
Aged				

BEHAVIOR MECHANISM RATING

Mechanism	High	Medium	Low
Gross Motor			
Manipulat.			
Verbal			
Affective			
Thinking			
Mood	Active	Normal	Passive

Figure 2.2 Observation schedule enables the recording of different types of information for different spaces in a building

Different types of furniture, equipment, and spatial characteristics will identify the activities for which particular spaces were designed.

- What might one need to know about the physical setting? Environmental cues help to define what types of activities might occur in a particular setting. Since settings may not have physical boundaries such as walls, it is possible that several settings might be located in a room, such as a childrens playroom with activity centers for math, science, reading, and dramatics.

To graphically explain how people use spaces, information recorded on data sheets can also be plotted on a floor plan of a building, or a site plan of an outdoor space. People's locations and activities are noted, as shown of Figure 2.3. Repeated observations are made the desired number of times. Individual observations can then be transferred onto one map to explain behavioral patterns of use. By preparing maps recorded at different time intervals, space use patterns can be compared to time. Determinations can then be made about conflicting activites, as well as the spatial distribution of activities.

Social mapping

Social mapping is a technique that enables one to explore and identify the social interactions that exist between people in a particular environment. It is an approach that consists of preferences and rejections expressed by individuals in terms of how they perceive themselves in relation to other members of the group. When the physical environment is considered in terms of its influence on social interactions, the spatial organization is one aspect that requires examination. Spatial organization can be viewed as the physical and functional distance between persons, groups, and activities (Wells, 1972). In addition, Moleski (1974) and others indicate that spatial organization can be looked upon as a communications network, an arrangement of parts that either helps or hinders social interaction and information flow. The sociogram (Moreno, 1934) is a graphic tool for describing friendship or interpersonal patterns that are obtained by asking questions such as , 'Who are your three best friends in the group?' In whom do you confide?' 'With whom do you enjoy working the most?' The sociogram can also provide data that begin to identify perceived authority structure in an organization's staff, and information flow or communications network that exist in a group.

The format for obtaining information to be graphically mapped consists of a series of questions requiring each respondent to rank order in terms of importance who affected him/her the most in the following ways:

- those authorized to pass on information, policy, and guidelines;
- those from whom they received the information vital to their position;
- those on the secretarial staff with whom they worked the most;
- those on the professional staff with whom they worked the most;
- those with whom they preferred to work;
- those who were influenced most by one's activities;
- those who influenced most one's own activites;
- those who were key decision makers.

Figure 2.3 A behavioral map shows the location of people in an environment, which may be an outdoor area, as shown, or different spaces in a building

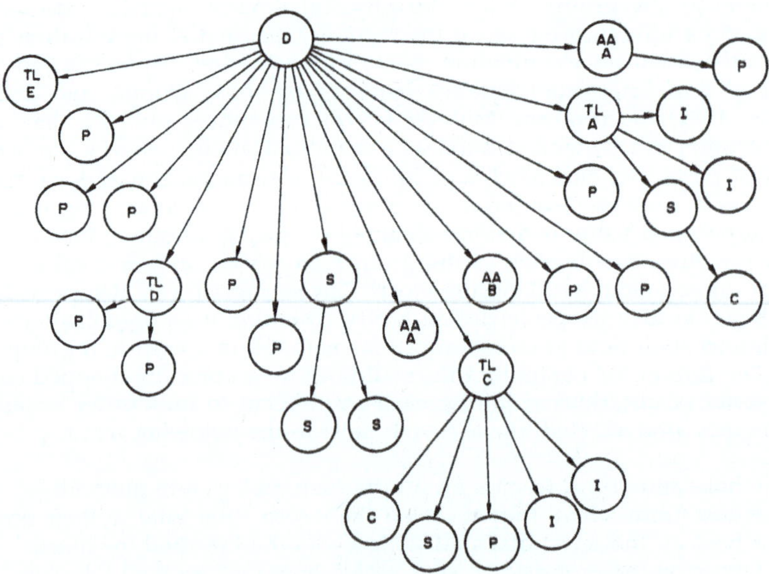

Figure 2.4 Example of a sociogram. Note large cluster around D, smaller clusters around TLD, S, TLC, and TLA. This is a ranking for the question: 'From whom do you receive information necesssary in the performance of your job?'

Sociograms can then be plotted for rankings to each question. The procedure for using the sociogram requires the identification of the critical issues to be studied, such as the actual influence of office size on social interaction. Specific questions need to be asked about friendship, about perceived authority, or about information flow. A reply sheet needs to be devised where preferences are ranked. And, finally, an adequate sample size should be determined. For organizations with fewer than forty people, each individual should be a respondent. A sociogram can then be plotted for each choice as shown in Figure 2.4. Based on the findings, the existing environment can be assessed, and a more responsive environment can be created through a spatial and/or social reorganization.

Visual assessment techniques

Appraisal measures the interaction between the human observer and the visual environment. Observer-based assessments of environmental quality consist of preferential judgements and comparative appraisals (Craik & Zube, 1976). Preferential judgements represent subjective reactions to specific environments, while comparative appraisals judge the quality of specific environments against a standard of comparison (Craik & McKechnie, 1974).

The environment can be represented by different modes. Although verbal descriptions have been used to represent the environment, direct and indirect methods decrease the possibility for misrepresentation. One method is to present the relevant features of the environment directly to observers. Direct representations may be made in the natural setting, thus minimizing opportunities for error when environments are represented by simulations.

Indirect representations are used most often and vary widely with the features of the environment being studied. Graphic representations are used where visually perceived properties of the environment are being assessed. Environmental images are usually presented, in the form of photographs (Figure 2.5) or slides, to subjects who rate them on a large number of rating scales.

An assessment technique to permit expressions of subtle reactions to the environment through verbal descriptions is a rating scale, referred to as a semantic differential (Osgood, Suci, & Tannenbaum, 1957). Descriptive judgements about the physical environment can be made by using a scale of opposite attributes. To be effective the scales should refer to the attributes of the environment rather than to subjective experiences. The verbal scale consists of pairs of attributes placed at opposite ends of a five step scale where each step represents different degrees of intensity (Figure 2.6).

There are three preliminary steps necessary prior to conducting a verbal assessment. First, a vocabulary of descriptive attributes must be prepared. Second, a method should be chosen for presenting the physical environment. Third, a group should be selected to participate in the study.

A variation in the development of descriptive attributes is the concept of personal constructs (Kelly, 1955). This approach relies on people's ability to form independent judgements that contain polar opposites (Figure 2.7).

BuildingImage: In the following section we are going to analyze different building facades with the purpose of defining the one that best suits the image of an arts center. Please answer all questions.	Please number the pictures below in rank order according to the image that best fits an art center.	Describe each of the five pictures.	What features do you particularly like in each of the five pictures?	What features do you particularly dislike in each of the five pictures?

Figure 2.5 Building image survey: Open ended responses and a ranking

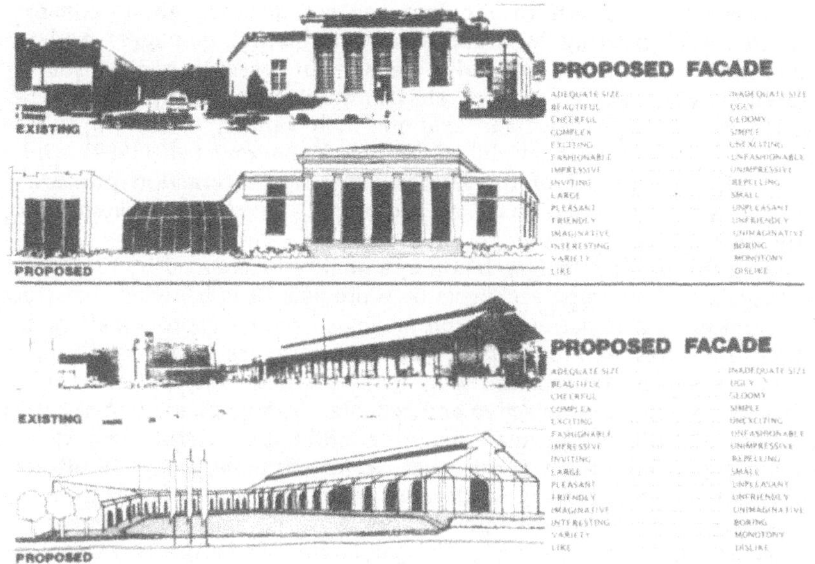

Figure 2.6 Building character studies using a polar opposite verbal scale

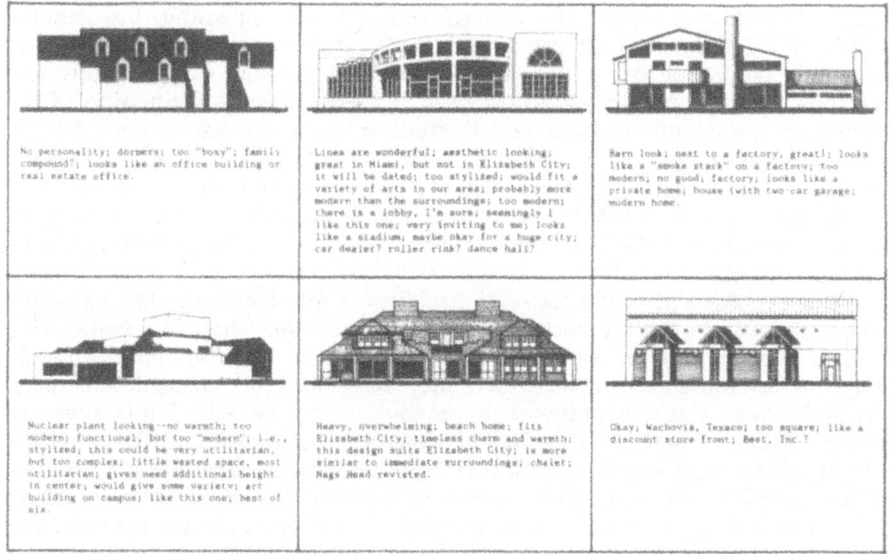

Figure 2.7 Building character study eliciting responses from the subjects

Landscape evaluation paradigms

With increasing concern in the last several decades about conserving, regulating, and creating landscapes, environmental managers and policy makers have searched for valid means of assessing the quality of comprehensive, visually natural environments. In attempting to classify various research approaches and examine their validity according to theory, testing, and representational ability, Taylor, Zube, and Sell (1987) applied a mutual influence model of the human-landscape interaction process. Four paradigms were identified based on the model: *expert, psychophysical, cognitive,* and *experiential.*

Using the *expert paradigm,* landscape quality is assessed by highly skilled experts such as landscape architects or ecologists. It is believed that through their training and experience, experts have become more sensitive to the aesthetic qualities of landscapes, and therefore are better qualified than ordinary people to appreciate them. It is assumed that professional judgements will also be more objective and reliable. Testing by the Forest Service is often done according to formal design or landscape criteria, such as boundaries and edges, land form, plant cover, water elements, and focal attractions; compositional types, feature landscape, enclosure, and focus (Litton, 1968); contrast, sequence, axis, convergence, codominance, and enframement.

According to the *psychophysical paradigm,* landscape is valued for its ability to stimulate responses in observers. Based upon traditional experimental psychology, psychophysical research measures the conditioned aesthetic response of observers to external and invariant properties of a landscape, which designers and managers can then manipulate in creating and enhancing environments. The approach has been used to broaden the base of landscape assessment to measure the aesthetic values of the general public: to determine what the general public finds appealing, the general public or a special interest group is tested. Much of the work in outdoor recreation landscape perception has been done according to psychophysical methods. Daniel and Boster (1976) used a Scenic Beauty Estimation (SBE) Method to ask respondents to rate thirty-five landscape scenes on a 1-to-10 scale. Pitt and Zube (1979) used the Q-sort method of having subjects place predetermined numbers of cards into separate piles according to degrees of scenic quality, to establish the importance of topographic relief, water, agricultural elements, natural elements, the context of cultural features, and land-use covers.

The key concept of the *cognitive paradigm* is that landscape has value for people because of the intellectual or social associations that they make with various settings. Rather than reacting passively to environmental stimuli, people select those aspects for which they have built up constructs, usually on the basis of visual experience. Researchers focus on why landscapes are valued, rather than what is valued. Various assumptions about the basis for selection have been tested, among them that preference is based on a optimal number, neither too many, nor too few, of features (Wohlwill & Kohn, 1976); that preference is shown for those aspects of environment that relate to the needs of the perceiver (Kaplan, 1979). Most research following the cognitive paradigm has been conducted using verbal response techniques - survey questions, adjective checklists, and semantic rating scales.

Work within the *experiential paradigm* studies landscape values derived from active human participation in the environment. The landscape acquires meaning through the situations in which it is experienced; as those situations change, the experiences and meanings change. Some researchers have examined the inspirational potential of landscape, its ability to produce 'sublime' or 'transcendent' experience, through verbal reports of their subjects. Others have focused on methods of enhancing the experience of landscapes by increasing sensitivity, and bases of appreciation through experience and knowledge.

Techniques used in measuring experiential values are less structured than those used in other paradigms. Because experience depends on the nature and intensity of the interaction of people and environment, most studies accept their subjects' subjective responses according to the personal criteria by which they were generated.

Taylor, Zube, and Sell (1987) suggest the benefits of combining paradigms in studying, managing, and designing the landscape. The expert view is suited to describing and documenting the physical components. Psychophysical studies can be used to identify those components which are most likely to be associated with scenic beauty, while the cognitive approach can provide understanding of the meaning and associations which observers attach to them. The experiential paradigm can be used to study and describe the interaction of landscapes and people, bringing together the landscape focus of the expert and psychophysical views, and the human focus of the cognitive.

Visual Appraisal

Another approach for developing a deeper understanding of the visual environment is a self-guided tour. Unlike other assessment strategies that rely upon conventional social science techniques for describing and judging the environment, the checklist offers individuals and groups a procedure for taking a structured walk through a building. This is an impressionistic approach which increases people's awareness of the environment by focusing on visual factors. The results of such a walk-through encourage responses about views, walkways, barriers, daylight, orientation, wayfinding, and appearance.

The CRIG analysis, developed by Bishop (1977), allows observers to appraise visual quality in terms of four key elements—*context, routes, interface,* and *grouping.* Any building or group of buildings is amenable to such appraisal. By using a series of checklist questions and a numerical rating scheme, scores are assigned to the factor being appraised. The process uses notes, drawings, and photographs to supplement the factors described in the checklist.

Numerical scores from 1 to 7 (1 = highly appropriate, 7 = highly inappropriate) are assigned to each question in the checklist. Individual scores are then averaged and an overall project score is assigned. An appraisal report would consider:

1. Description of the building(s) appraised with supportive illustrations (photographs, sketches, maps, diagrams).
2. Appraisal of the building(s) according to the four-factor analysis using the checklists, with responses and numerical scores for each question provided.
3. A paragraph describing the success or lack of success with which each factor is achieved or satisfied.
4. Analysis of numerical ratings by computation of average scores for each factor of the appraisal, and computation of the overall score for the building(s).
5. Concluding comments based upon the overall appraisal of the building(s).

Factor 1. CONTEXT: The building's setting

Highly appropriate 1 2 3 4 5 6 7 *Very inappropriate* Score

1. How does the building suit the pattern of the surrounding streets? ____
2. How does the scale of the building suit the site it sits upon? ____
3. How does the scale of the building suit the scale of surrounding buildings? ____
4. How does the scale suit the character of the neighborhood? ____
5. Do the public and private areas relate well to one another? ____
6. Do the land uses adjacent to the building seem to fit harmoniously with the building? ____
7. Do the type of building and its intended use fit well with the type and uses of adjacent buildings? ____
8. Does the appearance of the building fit well with the type of buildings surrounding it? ____
9. Is the scale of the building suitable for its purpose on the site? ____

Average Score (total/9) =

A summary paragraph should be written to express the observers' concerns about the way the building suits or fails to suit the context of the surrounding area. An example of such a summary is as follows:

> The site of the structure is the new Robson Square Complex located in the heart of downtown Vancouver. Four busy commercial streets—Howe, Smithe, Nelson and Hornby—surround the complex. A covered office walkway bridge connects the Law Courts to Robson Square by passing over Smithe Street.
>
> Instead of tall, narrow buildings rising vertically from the sidewalk, the architect has used an angled geometric structure for the building and has provided a considerable number of pedestrian walkways, grassy areas, trees, shrubs and water as well as seating areas. The Robson Square facility which connects to the Law Courts is a "people place" with gardens, private and public space, roller rinks, restaurants, an information center and a theatre complex. Other uses of surrounding land are mixed. The Law Courts are central to the city core with hotels, commercial office buildings, shops and restaurants located in buildings which are mostly in the 30-50 year age category and of mixed architctural features. Adjacent buildings such as the Hotel Vancouver and the old courthouse provide an interesting contrast with their unique and attractive architecture.

> The structure of the Law Court facility is so designed that different views of the surrounding building and of the structure itself are apparent from each level. The building, with its ample public space, allows access from adjacent streets and buildings and allows recreational and leisure time activity for the public as well as serving its intended function as a legal facility. (Davis, 1981)

Scores: (following completion of checklist on context) 4,2,1,1,2,2,3,2,2
Total = 19, Average = **2.1**

Factor 2. ROUTES: Routes are the traffic paths or passageways that allow the building to relate to its context

Highly appropriate 1 2 3 4 5 6 7 *Very inappropriate* Score

1. Are sufficient routes, pathways, streets, and passageways provided to and around the building? ____
2. What are the flow patterns of traffic or people? Are there busy periods, quiet periods, one-way flows, regular movement patterns, traffic jams? Are the routes arranged to consider these factors? ____
3. Where are the nodes (meeting points) for traffic around the building and what happens there? ____
4. Do all the routes make sense? Are they understandable and convenient? ____
5. Are all the routes easily understood by newcomers, visitors, service people? ____
6. How well are the routes marked? Are the markings clear and easily understood? ____
7. How effectively do the routes link the building to the surrounding buildings or structures? ____

Average Score (total/7) =

A summary paragraph should be written to describe the way in which the routes in and around the building(s) relate the building to its context and the success with which the routes accomplish that purpose.

Factor 3. INTERFACE: A building is essentially an enclosure that separates an interior private space from exterior public space. The interface is the crucial meeting place where the inside of the building connects with the outside.

Connections to outdoors: University of Sydney, School of Architecture (Photo: Henry Sanoff). *Interface:* There are a number of entrances at different street levels of the architecture school. Use of large glass areas provides ample light at entrances and corridors. The function of the building is apparent from its outside appearance. Although there are no signs informing visitors about the building's function, the large glass areas suggest the presence of studios. *Score: (from completion of interface checklist)* 5,2,2,3,2,1,4,3, = 23/8 = 2.9

Highly appropriate 1 2 3 4 5 6 7 *Very inappropriate* Score

1. How clearly or effectively does the exterior of the building indicate its interior function(s)? ____
2. How effectively does the exterior of the building connect with the outside of the building? Are the connections appropriate and functional? ____
3. Are the exits and entrances easily accessible? ____
4. Are the various openings related to thoughtful planning of the interior? (Consider entry of light, view, privacy, noise, heat, glare, atmosphere, etc.) ____
5. Are the exitways appropriate from a safety point of view? ____

6. When you move from the exterior of the building to the interior by means of the main entrance, is the experience pleasant, interesting, or special in any way? ____
7. Are the clues to what is public and what is private space clear to the visitor? ____
8. Have the designers, in your opinion, handled the problem of interface well in their design of this building? ____

Average Score (total/8) =

A summary paragraph should be written describing how well the design of the building has addressed the problem of interface, including the strengths and weaknesses of the design, and how it might be improved.

Factor 4. GROUPING: Buildings are usually divided into sections which are organized in form into some type of grouping. Grouping of the parts gives both form and meaning as well as variety to the building.

Highly appropriate 1 2 3 4 5 6 7 *Very inappropriate* Score

1. Concentrate on the subdivision of the building's parts as viewed from the outside. What parts are evident? Do the parts integrate well with each other and form an effective and pleasing appearance? ____
2. Do the subdivided parts of the building appear to have a specific function? Is the function of each part easy to identify? ____
3. Is it clear what various subdivisions of the building might mean to visitors? Would a visitor know where to go on entering the building? ____
4. Are the various parts of the building planned carefully in relation to one another and to the characteristics of the site? ____
5. Is there sufficient relationship between the parts of the building for it to appear as one unified structure? ____
6. Does enough variation exist in the structural parts and groupings to provide interest and variety? ____

Average Score (total/6) =

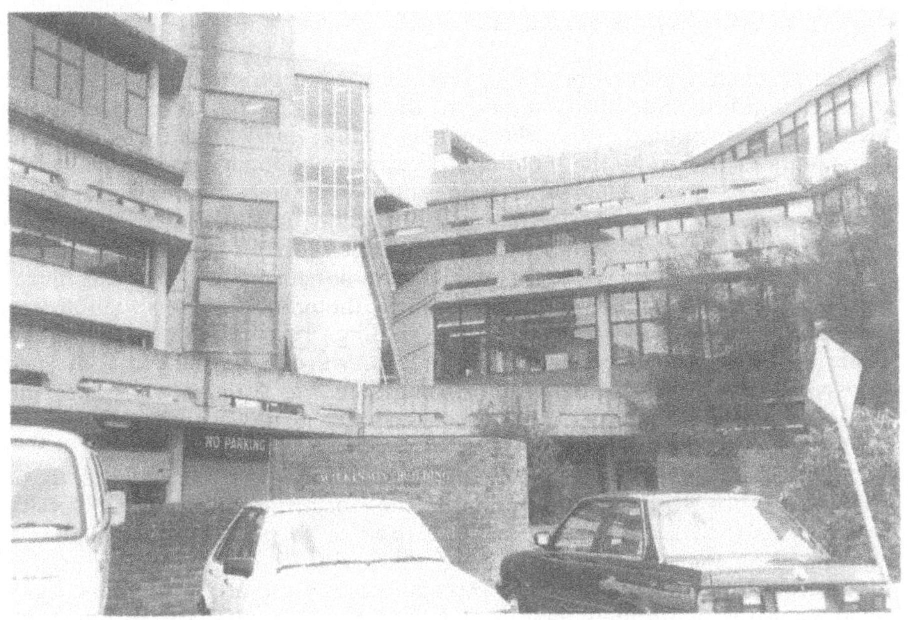

Massing of building elements: University of Sydney, School of Architecture (Photo: Henry Sanoff). *Groupings:* Viewed from the campus entrance, the architecture school creates an intersecting massing of building elements. From the city street, the visitor enters through a door into a walled court, providing a different face to the street than to the campus. Circulation within the building is interrupted by a two-story space which redirects movement through studio areas.

A summary paragraph should be written to discuss the building's subdivision into identifiable parts, the way those parts are grouped, and how successfully the concept of grouping was employed.

Finally, a synopsis of the assessment might be:

> An extremely interesting structure that combines public space and interest with an important community and government function in a unique and creative way. To the visitor, function and routes of access may be somewhat obscure, however the uniqueness and versatility of the design, which is appealing, prove to be a significant factor in the apraisal (Davis, p. 37).

Open plan office evaluation: A case study

A post-occupancy evaluation (POE) was carried out on a recently completed campus building. The study aimed to document the nature of user satisfaction in an open plan office. The impetus behind this POE was the frequent complaints registered by the building's occupants about comfort and privacy.

A questionnaire was developed and administered to the staff and managers of both floors of this addition. The questions tried to elicit responses to office workability and performance as they related to conditions of comfort and privacy. While the results were not surprising, they did reveal considerable dissatisfaction with the building, though the social situation was cconsidered to be quite agreeable. The findings provided the quantitative evidence that the previous complaints were neither random nor idiosyncratic. As a result a livibility committee was formed to explore the range of possible modifications necessary to achieve higher levels of satisfaction.

The project aimed to confirm suspicions about user dissatisfaction in an open plan office building. An addition to the North Carolina State University campus designed for a maximum population of 50 people, Ricks Hall is a building housing components of the Agricultural Extension Service. It functions as an office building and incorporates the use of partitionless, open planning office equipment layout (Figure 2.8). This 4300 sq. ft. building, designed in 1981 by Wolf Associates Architects, was constructed of brick exterior walls with a concrete floor and exposed concrtete roof system. It is separated from old Ricks Hall by a courtyard walkthrough exposing the new addition to the old facade by a continuous wall of clear glass. The work spaces were designed using low dividers to separate the various staff personnel.

Client

The results of a recent North Carolina legislative act oriented towards combining higher education programs created the need for additional office space for the Agricultural Extension Service at the North Carolina State University campus. A team of departmental representatives was designated as the building committee by the Director. In conjunction with the Division of Campus Planning, who offered technical advice, the client group devised a plan to add an additional floor to the current Ricks Hall building. Based on the space available on the proposed floor a budget was established and an architect selected. Before proceeding, the architect requested extensive testing of the existing building to ensure that it would be able to support an additional floor. The potential cost of the tests was so high that the building committee suggested that other alternatives should be explored. Since the current building contained typical closed offices, the architect proposed an open plan alternative in order to allow a wider range of activities to occur. The building committee was not convinced that the open plan suited their projected needs, however, the school director made an unpopular decision by supporting the architect's proposal for a two story, open plan office building.

An earlier version of this paper appeared in *Design Studies*, 6,4 (1985): 187-195.

Process

A relatively new innovation in office planning originated in West Germany called 'Burolandschaff,' or the open office plan, is a landscaping concept based on the integration between the organizational process and the physical grouping of people who work together (Starbuck, 1976). Fixed partitions are eliminated in favor of spatially organized work groups. The open design approach claims to have greater staff productivity, reduction in space requirements, decrease in maintenance costs, reduction in set up and renovation time, and improved staff morale and decreased absenteeism.

With the high cost of real estate, the many advantages claimed for the open landscape approach attracted considerable attention. Many large organizations such as Kodak, Port Authority of New York, McDonald's Corporation, and others have installed landscaped offices. However, upon some investigation, it appeared that there was a lack of evidence to support these claims. In a survey of Kodak's employees, Riland (1970) concluded that although the atmosphere improved, the landscape was too public and comfort control was difficult to achieve. The Port Authority of New York (Zetlin, 1969) commissioned a comprehensive study of their office environment which failed to reveal any advantages in the office landscape concept that could not be achieved in an equivalent designed environment in a conventional office. The study further pointed out that despite the extreme change in the physical environment from a bad conventional office to a good landscaped office, attitudinal changes about the job changed minimally. More recent surveys of user reactions to landscaped or open plan offices have highlighted complaints of loss of privacy, high incidence of visual and aural distractions, frequent interruptions by other employees, and problems with ambient conditions (Wineman, 1982; Marans and Spreckelmeyer, 1982; and Hedge, 1982). The feelings against open plan offices are so strong that this approach has been abandoned in the Netherlands, and similar attitudes persist in Germany. In spite of the controversy, many organizations in the U.S.A. and in the U.K. remain committed to the concept of open plan offices. Although it was not our purpose to prove or disprove these claims attributed to the office landscape, this POE study was undertaken to explore employee attitudes about their work environment, particularly as they affect work conditions and human comfort.

A 31 item questionnaire was prepared and administered to 26 occupants of the building (Figure 2.10). Survey respondents were a group of predominantly female (79%) office workers, over the age of 35 (80%), nearly half of whom indicated that almost all of their time at work was spent at their own work station. Questions typically were of the 'closed' format, in which respondents were asked to indicate one of four or five possible answers. Additionally, a technique was developed that required the workers to respond to a number of environmental adjectives by indicating on two, three point scales, the extent to which (a) each adjective described their workplace, and (b) the relative sufficiency of this characteristic in their environment. Finally, two open- ended questions asked each respondent to indicate three job related likes and dislikes. Although the focus of the survey was on thermal and daylighting conditions, a number of other environmental characteristics (e.g. noise level) were considered. While only the most robust findings will be discussed here, the complete results are given in Tables 2.1 to 2.9.

Nearly three-fourths of the workers reported that temperature and ventilation conditions were 'rarely satisfactory' as shown in Table 2.1. Further, 62% (Table 2.2) believed that this sometimes led to job performance problems, while 93% indicated that thermal conditions caused them to feel less satisfied with their jobs (Table 2.3). When the work area was too warm or too cool, the actions reported by the respondents to improve conditions fell into two different behavioral categories. One action behavior was 'adaptive' where one-half of the employees reported that they would add or remove clothing or work elsewhere in the building. Another reported behavior was 'complaintive' where discomfort was reported to the maintenance staff or the supervisor.

In contrast, the lighting/outside view/window characteristics were regarded with favor. These variables, in fact, were the most frequently cited when employees were asked to list those things they liked best in their workplace, as shown in Table 2.4. Further, of all the environmental descriptors, 'light' was most strongly categorized as being 'just right.' Almost half (46%) of the respondents (Table 2.5) felt that the presence of daylight never inhibited their job performance, while more than two-thirds believed that such light usually increased their level of overall job satisfaction (Table 2.6).

Support for the validity of this technique may be found by comparing these results with the open-ended questions where respondents were asked to list three major things they liked and three things they disliked about their office. As previously detailed, close agreement was found in responses to lighting conditions as determined through these two techniques. Similarly, noise level headed the list of major dislikes in the workplace, and 'noise' was to the greatest degree reported 'too much,' and 'quiet' to the least degree, reported 'not enough.'

The next greatest insufficiency indicated was for 'privacy' while 'open' was the next characteristic rated 'too much.' These were in agreement with lack of walls and privacy being the second most often reported dislike with this environment. Similar comparisons were made for rankings of 'adaptable,' 'orderly' and/or 'efficient' on the adjective item with complaints of insufficient or inefficient use of space for work, and storage in the open-ended question (See Table 2.7).

In summary, it would appear that noise, privacy, and thermal conditions in Ricks Hall Annex were considered by employees to be serious problems and similar to those cited by Zeitlin and Riland. These conditions were felt to lessen worker satisfaction as well as to reduce worker performance levels. In contrast, the large expanse of window area was by-and-large regarded favorably. A problem was that while one-third of the employees believed that the most important advantage of a window was to admit fresh air into the space, the windows in Ricks Hall Annex were sealed, a factor listed by several workers among their major dislikes. When asked about the view from the window, only one-third of the respondents described it as satisfying (Table 2.8). Broadly speaking, 71% of the survey respondents (Table 2.9) felt that the physical environment in which they worked was worse than that provided in other offices.

Table 2.1

TEMPERATURE AND VENTILATION CONDITIONS

	Number	Percentage
Always satisfactory	0	0
Usually satisfactory	6	23
Rarely satisfactory	19	73
Never satisfactory	1	4

Table 2.2

TEMPERATURE AND VENTILATION CONDITIONS AND JOB PERFORMANCE

	Number	Percentage
Always lead to job performance problems	0	0
Frequently lead to job performance problems	8	30
Sometimes lead to job performance problems	16	62
Never lead to job performance problems	2	8

Table 2.3

TEMPERATURE AND VENTILATION CONDITIONS AND JOB SATISFACTION

	Number	Percentage
Usually increase your overall job satisfaction	0	0
Sometimes increase your overall job satisfaction	0	0
Have no effect on your overall job satisfaction	2	7
Sometimes decrease your overall job satisfaction	20	77
Usually decrease your overall job satisfaction	4	16

Table 2.4

LIKES AND DISLIKES ABOUT THE OFFICE LANDSCAPE

LIKES		DISLIKES	
Natural lighting/ view/ windows	9	Noise/ distractions	22
Plants	6	Lack of walls/ privacy	15
Co-workers	6	Temperature/ ventilation	12
Decor/ furnishings	5	Insufficient work/ storage space	12
Proximity to co-workers	2	Decor/ furnishings	3
Space for personalization	1	Sealed windows	3
Openness	1	Limited view	2
Working conditions	1	Lack of necessary equipment	1
Quiet	1	Exterior connection with old building	1
Convenient	1	Excessive distance to co-workers	1
Accessible	1		

Table 2.5

PRESENCE OF DAYLIGHT AND JOB PERFORMANCE

	Number	Percentage
Usually increase your overall job satisfaction	12	46
Sometimes increase your overall job satisfaction	0	0
Have no effect on your overall job satisfaction	10	38
Sometimes decrease your overall job satisfaction	4	16
Usually decrease your overall job satisfaction	0	0

Table 2.6

PRESENCE OF DAYLIGHT AND JOB SATISFACTION

	Number	Percentage
Always lead to job performance problems	0	0
Frequently lead to job performance problems	3	12
Sometimes lead to job performance problems	5	20
Never lead to job performance problems	18	68

Table 2.7

ENVIRONMENTAL REACTION SCALE

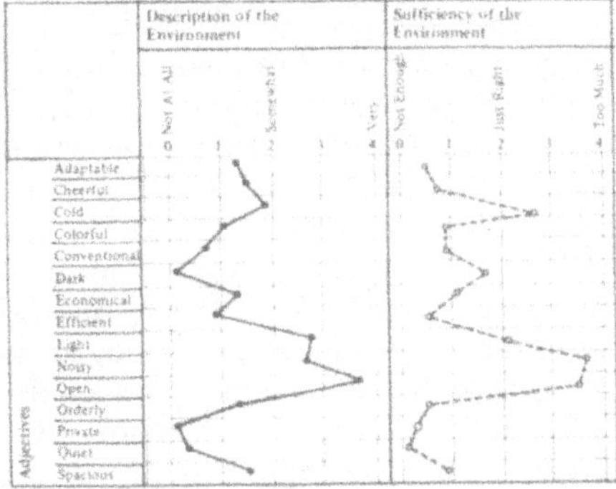

Table 2.8

VIEW FROM THE WINDOW

	Number	Percentage
Unpleasant	0	0
Dull	5	21
Limited	11	46
Satisfying	7	29
Appealing	1	4
Stimulating	0	0

Table 2.9

DESCRIPTION OF THE OVERALL PHYSICAL ENVIRONMENT

	Number	Percentage
Much worse than other places	7	29
Somewhat worse than other places	10	42
About the same as other places	5	21
Slightly better than other places	1	4
Much better than other places	1	4

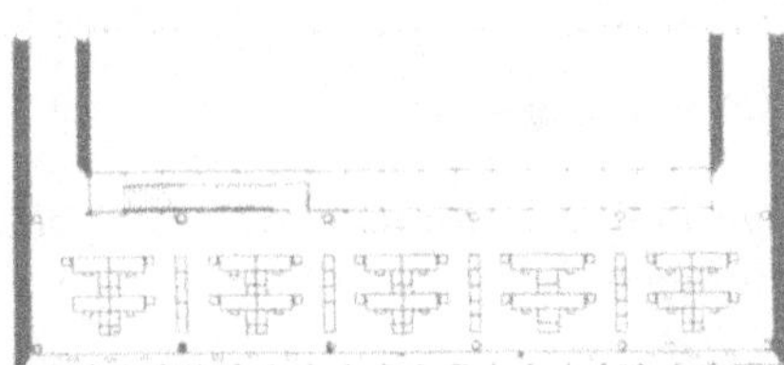

First Floor Plan

Implementation

The evaluation study provided the quantitative evidence that there were problems requiring immediate attention. It was apparent that this systematic approach to identifying levels of user satisfaction had considerable impact beyond the individual complaints previously addressed to the management. As a result, the Ricks Hall Livability Committee was formed to identify corrective measures.

The first major physical modification to the building was the installation of an acoustic ceiling on the second floor. Occupants agreed that it reduced the noise level considerably, but not to the point of satisfaction. This modification was made by the University's maintenance servicers without review by or consultation with the Division of Campus Planning's architectural staff. Since it was apparent that acoustic ceilings rarely solve noise transmission problems, other more effective alternatives might have been explored such as changing the use of the area that would be more conducive to open space planning.

The second major revision to the building was to change the entire use of the ground floor, as suggested by the University architect, from an administrative/clerical function to the art department where noise and privacy were not critical factors to their work process. In order to create usable layout space for the art staff, floor to ceiling partitions replaced the four foot high space dividers on the floor. This provided well defined work areas, where the open corridor was appropriate for the type of traffic flow between work areas (Figure 2.9). Since the original scheme intended to use the space between the free-standing columns and the exterior wall for visitors waiting, this area has now evolved into a storage area because the new use precludes the need for waiting.

Acknowledgment

The initial evaluation study was conducted with the cooperation of Dr. Dan Pond and Graham Adams.

Figure 2.8 Office interior after initial occupancy

Figure 2.9 Office interior changes after evaluation study

The following questions ask about your feelings and reactions to the physical environment in your work place. Your answers are completely confidential, and will be used only as a part of a research effort to determine the best conditions for working people.

Unless otherwise instructed, you are to indicate only one choice for each question.

Thank you for your cooperation.

Check One

1. In general, what portion of each work day do you spend in your office or at your own work station?

[ ] 80 - 100%
[ ] 60 - 80%
[ ] 40 - 60%
[ ] 20 - 40%
[ ] 0 – 20%

2. How many co-workers share this office or work station with you?

[ ] 0
[ ] 1
[ ] 2
[ ] 3 - 6
[ ] more than 6

3. In general, what portion of each day will be spent with visitors or clients in your immediate work area?

[ ] 80 - 100%
[ ] 60 - 80%
[ ] 40 - 60%
[ ] 20 - 40%
[ ] 0 – 20%

4. Considering the number of co-workers and visitors in your office or work station, would you say that this area is:

[ ] Much too small
[ ] A bit too small
[ ] Just about right
[ ] A bit too large
[ ] Much too large

5. In hot weather, is the temperature of your office or work station

[ ] Cold
[ ] Cool
[ ] Slightly cool
[ ] Comfortable
[ ] Slightly warm
[ ] Warm
[ ] Hot

6. In cold weather, is the temperature of your office or work station

[ ] Cold
[ ] Cool
[ ] Slightly cool
[ ] Comfortable
[ ] Slightly warm
[ ] Warm
[ ] Hot

7. Does the amount of air movement in your workplace make the area:

[ ] Frequently too drafty
[ ] Occasionally too drafty
[ ] Just about right
[ ] Occasionally too stuffy
[ ] Frequently too stuffy

8. On days when your workplace is too warm or stuffy, which of the following actions do you use to improve conditions: (Check only those which apply)

[ ] It never becomes too warm or stuffy
[ ] Adjust thermostat
[ ] Wear less or remove clothing
[ ] Open windows or door
[ ] Call in sick or go home early
[ ] Call maintenance staff
[ ] Work elsewhere in the building
[ ] Complain to supervisor
[ ] Other (please specify)

9. On days when your workplace is too cool or drafty, which of the following actions do you use to improve conditions (Check only those which apply)

[ ] It never becomes too warm or stuffy
[ ] Adjust thermostat
[ ] Wear more or add clothing
[ ] Close windows or doors
[ ] Call in sick or go home early
[ ] Call maintenance staff
[ ] Work elsewhere in building
[ ] Complain to supervisor
[ ] Other (please specify)

10. Are the temperature and ventilation conditions in your work area?

[ ] Always satisfactory
[ ] Usually satisfactory
[ ] Rarely satisfactory
[ ] Never satisfactory

11. Do the temperature and ventilation conditions in your work area:

[ ] Always lead to job performance problems
[ ] Frequently lead to job performance problems
[ ] Sometimes lead to job performance problems
[ ] Never lead to job performance problems

12. Do the temperature and ventilation conditions in your work area:

[ ] Usually increase your overall job satisfaction
[ ] Sometimes increase your overall job satisfaction
[ ] Have no effect on your overall job satisfaction
[ ] Sometimes decrease your overall job satisfaction
[ ] Usually decrease your job overall job satisfaction

14. How important is it to you to have a source of natural light (for example, a window or a skylight) in your work area?

[ ] Very important
[ ] Moderately important
[ ] Unimportant
[ ] Would rather have none

15. What type or combination of light do you prefer to work by?

[ ] Daylight
[ ] Artificial light
[ ] Daylight and artificial light combined
[ ] No preference

16. What type of lighting is used in your work area?

[ ] Daylight
[ ] Artificial light
[ ] Daylight and artificial light combined
[ ] No preference

13. For each of the following adjectives please indicate:

A) To what degree does each word describe your work place, | and B) in what amount is this characteristic present in your work place

Example						
Dull	○	●	○	○	●	○
	Not At All	Somewhat	Very	Not Enough	Just Right	Too Much
Adaptable	○	○	○	○	○	○
Cheerful	○	○	○	○	○	○
Cold	○	○	○	○	○	○
Colorful	○	○	○	○	○	○
Conventional	○	○	○	○	○	○
Dark	○	○	○	○	○	○
Economical	○	○	○	○	○	○
Efficient	○	○	○	○	○	○
Light	○	○	○	○	○	○
Noisy	○	○	○	○	○	○
Open	○	○	○	○	○	○
Orderly	○	○	○	○	○	○
Private	○	○	○	○	○	○
Quiet	○	○	○	○	○	○
Spacious	○	○	○	○	○	○

17. Please indicate which advantage of windows you consider to be the most important in a workplace. (Check one)

[ ] None
[ ] Lets you see what's going on
[ ] Enables fresh air to enter
[ ] Makes the room appear more spacious
[ ] Provides a change of view or a break in the monotony
[ ] Other (please specify)

18. Do you think your present lighting arrangement provides: (Check one)

[ ] Too much daylight
[ ] Too much artificial light
[ ] Not enough daylight
[ ] Not enough artificial light
[ ] Satisfactory amounts of both types of light

19. Does the presence (or would the presence) of daylight in your work area

[ ] Always lead to job performance problems
[ ] Frequently lead to job performance problems
[ ] Sometimes lead to job performance problems
[ ] Never lead to job performance problems

20. Does the presence (or would the presence) of daylight in your work area:

[ ] Usually increase your overall job satisfaction
[ ] Sometimes increase your overall job satisfaction
[ ] Have no effect on your overall job satisfaction
[ ] Sometimes decrease your overall job satisfaction
[ ] Usually decrease your overall job satisfaction

21. Which of the following do you think is the most serious problem caused by windows in a work place? (Check one)

[ ] None
[ ] Allows area to be affected by outside temperatures
[ ] Causes glare
[ ] Reduces privacy
[ ] Allows distractions to enter
[ ] Makes the area drafty
[ ] Other (please specify)

22. Is glare from some artificial light source a problem for you?

[ ] Frequently
[ ] Sometimes
[ ] Rarely
[ ] Never

23. Do you have a window in your office or work station?

[ ] No (If no, skip to question 24)
[ ] Yes (If yes, please answer the following)

23.A How far would you estimate your typical work position to be from the nearest window?

[ ] Less than 5 feet
[ ] 5 to 15 feet
[ ] 16 to 25 feet
[ ] more than 25 feet

23.B How often do you choose to work using the light from the window?

[ ] Whenever possible
[ ] Sometimes
[ ] Never
[ ] Unable to control

23.C How often does the sunlight coming into your work area result in temperature problems?

[ ] Frequently
[ ] Sometimes
[ ] Rarely
[ ] Never

23.D Is the noise level near the window ever noticably greater than that in other parts of the work area?

[ ] Frequently
[ ] Sometimes
[ ] Rarely
[ ] Never

23.E Please check one term which best describes the view from your window:

[ ] Unpleasant
[ ] Dull
[ ] Limited
[ ] Satisfying
[ ] Appealing
[ ] Stimulating

23.F Are you able to open and close some part of the window area?

[ ] Yes
[ ] No

23.G Are drafts in your work area a problem for you?

[ ] Frequently
[ ] Sometimes
[ ] Rarely
[ ] Never

23.H Is glare from sunlight coming through the window a problem for you?

[ ] Frequently
[ ] Sometimes
[ ] Rarely
[ ] Never

24. What is your age?

[ ] Less than 20
[ ] 20 - 35
[ ] 36 - 50
[ ] 51 - 65
[ ] Greater than 65

25. Which sex are you?

[ ] Male
[ ] Female

26. How long have you been working at your present work station or office?

[ ] Less than 3 months
[ ] 3 months - 1 year
[ ] 1 - 5 years
[ ] More than 5 years

27. Is your office or work station located:

[ ] Below street level
[ ] At street level
[ ] 1 - 4 floors above street level
[ ] More than 4 floors above street level

28. Which of the following activities are frequently performed by you while at your own office or work station? (Check only those which apply)

[ ] Reading
[ ] Writing, transcribing, or drawing
[ ] Typing, photocoping, or calculating
[ ] Filing or storing material
[ ] Telephoning
[ ] Interviewing or conversing
[ ] Operating large machines (offset press, binding machinery, etc.)
[ ] Other (please specify)

29. In comparison to other places in which the work you do is performed, do you think the overall physical environment here is

[ ] Much worse than other places
[ ] Somewhat worse than other places
[ ] About the same as other places
[ ] Slightly better than other places
[ ] Much better than other places

30. Please list three major things that you like about your work place:

31. Please list three major things that you dislike about your work place:

Figure 2.10 Office evaluation questionnaire

3 Participatory design

Introduction

During the last two decades there has been a considerable movement towards the direct involvement of the public in the definition of their physical environment. The increased sense of social responsibility took root in the mid-1960's, when a new feeling of community consciousness started prevailing in many low income urban neighborhoods.

The term participation has come to cover a number of factors as it applies to group interactions. The recent meaning of participation defines it as face-to-face interaction of individuals who share a number of values important to all, that is to say a purpose for them being together. Participation will be a major aspect in a society in which the freedom of all citizens, in all aspects of social life, is well assured.

The effects of participation in the culture and the society have been pointed out by Davidoff (1965) who states that participation 'reduces the feeling of anonynimity and communicates to the users a greater degree of concern on the part of management or administration.' Furthermore, participation, is seen as an inclusive process where the planner or designer should represent the special interest group, just as a lawyer would represent his client's interest in court (Jencks, 1971). In this respect, participation is a matter of control over decisions.

People need to participate in the creation of their environment, they need the feeling of control; it is the only way that their needs and values can be taken into consideration. Participation is a means of protecting the interests of groups of people as well as of individuals, because it satisfies their needs which are very often totally or partially ignored by organizations, institutions, bureaucracies, and the 'expert' planners and designers.

With the introduction of the users in the decision-making process, designers have to add new capacities to their conventional experience. It does not mean that their creativity has been obliterated. Designers need to face the problem of balance between, not only what administration wishes, and what individual user groups desire, but also what seems best in terms of allocation of limited community resources.

Current views of participation

There has also emerged a new pragmatic approach to participation, one that no longer views participation as Arnstein's (1969) categorical term for 'citizen power.' The purposes of participation have been more modestly defined to include information exchange, resolving conflicts, and to supplement planning and design. '(Participation) reduces the feeling of anonymity and communicates to the user a greater degree of concern on the part of the management of administration. (With) it, residents are actively involved in the development process, there will be a better maintained physical environment, greater public spirit, more user satisfaction and significant financial savings' (Becker, 1977). Participation has a different meaning to different people and even a different meaning to the same people according to the situation. Participation has been stimulated by the communication revolution which has made people more aware of the problems associated with organizations. The two main purposes of participation are:

1. to involve people in design decision making processes and, as a result increase their trust and confidence in organizations, making it more likely that they will accept decisions and plans and work within the systems when seeking solutions to problems.

2. to provide people with a voice in design and decision-making in order to improve plans, decisions and service delivery.

An important point in the participatory process is individual learning through increased awareness of a problem. In order to maximize learning the process should be clear, communicable and open. It should encourage dialogue, debate and collaboration. This learning process is valuable to both users and designers.

The types and degrees of participation depend on several factors and vary in accord with the circumstances. For Alexander (1972), '..the most modest kind of participation is the kind where the user helps to shape a building by acting as a client of an architect. The fullest kind of participation is the kind where users actually build their building for themselves.'

Jim Burns (1979) classifies participation in four categories or 'experiences' that can lead to agreement about what the future should bring:

Awareness. This experience involves discovering or re-discovering the realities of a given environment of a situation so that everyone in the 'Take Part' process is talking the same language based on their experiences in the field where change is proposed.

Perception. This entails going from awareness of the situation to understanding it, and its physical, social, cultural and economic ramifications. It means sharing with each other so that the understanding, objectives, and expectations of all participants become resources for planning, and not hidden agendas that could disrupt the project later on. **Decison-making.** This phase concentrates on working from awareness and perception to a program for the situation under consideration. In it, participants make actual physical designs based on their priorities for professionals to use as resource to synthesize alternative and final plans. **Implementation.** Many community-based planning processes stop with awareness, perception and decision-making, often with fatal results to a project because it ends people's responsibilities just when they could be of most value: when the how-to, where-to, when-to, and who-will-do-it must be added to what people want and how it will look. People must stay involved, throughout the processes, in other words, and take responsibility with their professionals to see that there are results (Hurwitz, 1975).

Purposes of participation

Participation from the Latin 'pars', a part, means to be and to act as a part of a larger order of a higher totality or wholeness (Schmid, 1985). Participation refers to the fact or conditions of sharing in common with others, and refers to making decisions with regards to the common good. Participation implies the presence of the users during the whole course of the architectural operation which passes through three phases; the definition of the problem, the elaboration of the solution, and the evaluation of the results (De Carlo,1980). Participation has a number of synonyms, such as citizen involvement, citizen influence, citizen action groups, cooperation, co-decision, and self-decision. This implies that participation is a general concept covering different forms of decision-making by a number of involved parties (Wulz, 1985).

Participation, is a concept laden with ideology and assumptions. Often the arguments made for participation are not based on a clear conceptual understanding nor an appropriate organizing framework. Important issues in any framework must include factors such as who is participating, how people are participating, and what are the effects of participation.

Although the citizen participation mandate proliferates at all levels of government, those with the responsibility for design, implementation, and evaluation of participation programs have been given little guidance. Most mandates are vague and ambiguous. Rarely do they contain hints as to what is expected. Standards by which participation should be measured are conspicuous by their absence. There is little consistency in the way participation is perceived, in the way participation programs are developed, in the way participation programs are carried out, and in the way participation evaluations are performed. Therefore it is difficult to know what works and what doesn't, and opportunities to learn from the experiences of others have been severely limited.

Participation means different things to different people and different things to the same people, depending on the issue, its timing, and the political setting in which it takes place. Participation can be addressed effectively if the task of participation is conceptualized in terms of what is to be accomplished when the need is acknowledged to involve citizens. Conceptualizing the issue means asking simple questions of who, what, where, how, and when?

- Who are the parties to be involved in participation?
- What do we wish to have performed by the participation program?
- Where do we wish the participation road to lead?
- How should people be involved?
- When in the planning process is participation needed or desired?

These are simple questions, yet rarely are they asked prior to the development of a participatory design program.

It is necessary to realize is that user participation is like a professional sport. It takes place in a public forum where there is competition between individuals and groups with conflicting goals; where the individuals and groups that participate play different roles at different times; where the playing conditions change from time to time; where the planning of strategies is a major activity; where no one group wins every contest; and where there is an ongoing need to evaluate performance in order to succeed. Like the manager of a professional sports club, the designer of a participation program needs to think about goals and objectives, about options and plays, resources and timing, strategy and performances. And, like sports, planning for a successful participation program involves a great deal of thought and analysis prior to the first public performance. The planning that accompanies the design of any participation program should first include a determination of goals and objectives. For example:

- Is the participation intended to generate ideas?
- Is it to identify attitudes?
- Is it to disseminate information?
- Is it to resolve some identified conflict?
- It is to review a proposal?
- Or, is it merely to serve as a safety valve for pent-up emotions?

The list of possible participation objectives will differ from time to time and from issue to issue. Once the goals and objectives of participation are stated, it becomes clear that participation is perceived differently depending on the type of issue and people involved. If differences in perception and expectations are not identified at the outset, and realistic objectives are not made clear, the expectations of those involved in the participation program will not have been met, and they will become disenchanted. One of the stumbling blocks to an effective participation program is the difficulty associated with the articulation of participation goals and objectives. Yet it is this articulation that forms the basis of any wise choice of participation methods. The difficulty in determining goals, objectives, and methods may be caused by confusion over what is meant by planning a participation program (Rosner, 1978).

A *goal* is nothing more than a generalized statement of intended accomplishment.It is usually abstract and somewhat ambiguous. An ***objective*** is more specific. It is a statement of the changes on conditions that some activity is expected to produce; put another way, it is a function to be performed. A method is the vehicle by which an objective is to be achieved.

When participation goals and objectives are not clearly articulated, participants will have different expectations of what participation is to achieve. Many administrators find the involvement of users time consuming, inefficient, irrational and not very productive. However, when the purposes are made clear, then it is possible to plan activities that are directly related to the objectives. Examples of objectives would be:

To disseminate information.
To solicit and identify the attitudes and opinions of user groups.
To facilitate participation.
To generate new ideas and alternatives.
To establish priorities.

These objectives would be the functions to be performed by some set of participation activities. They constitute the purposes of participation.

Planning for the participation needs considerable time prior to the taking of any action. When sufficient time is allowed to analyze issues, participants, resources, and participation goals and objectives prior to the choosing of participation methods, the chance of success is greatly enhanced. The steps to successful participation planning are (Rosner, 1978):

- Identify the individuals or groups who will or should be involved in the participation activity being planned.
- Decide where in the planning process the participants should be involved; that is in development, implementation, evaluation or some combination thereof.
- Articulate the participation objectives in relation to all participants
- Identify participation methods to objectives in terms of the resources available.
- Match alternative methods to objectives in terms of the resources available.
- Select an appropriate method to be used in the achievement of specified objectives.
- Implement chosen participation activities.
- Evaluate the implemented methods to see to what extent they achieved the desired goals and objectives.

It is not suggested that taking the eight proposed steps will automatically ensure success, but it can be claimed that the process will minimize failure. A collective review of the theories and practices of participation are synthesized into the following five statements:

1. *There is no 'best solution' to design problems.* Each problem has a number of solutions. Solutions to design and planning problems are traditionally based on two sets of criteria: (a) ***facts***-- the empirical data concerning material strengths, economics, building codes, and so forth; and (b) ***attitudes***--interpretation of the facts, the state of the art in any particular area, traditional and customary approaches, and value judgements. Thus design and planning decisions are by nature biased and depend on the values of the decision maker(s).

2. *'Expert' decisions are not necessarily better than 'lay' decisions.* Given the facts with which to make decisions, the users can examine the available alternatives and choose among them. The architect, involved in such an approach, is a participant who is expected to state an opinion, provide technical information, and discuss consequences of various alternatives, just as the users state opinions and contribute their expertise.

3. *A design or planning task can be made 'transparent.'* Those steps taken and alternatives considered by the architect traditionally in their own minds in the privacy of an office can be brought to the surface for the users to discuss. By understanding the components of design decisions and 'shopping' among the alternatives, the users in effect generate their own plan rather than react to one provided for them. The final product is more likely to succeed because it is better understood by the people who will use it.

4. *All individuals and interest groups should come together in an open forum.* In this way people can openly express their opinions, make necessary compromises, and arrive at decisions that are acceptable to all concerned. By involving as many interests as possible, not only is the product strengthened by the wealth of input, but the user group is strengthened as well by learning more about itself.

5. *The process is continuous and ever changing.* The product is not the end of the process. It must be managed, re-evaluated, and adapted to changing needs. Those most directly involved with the product, the users, are best able to assume those tasks.

As a summary, four essential purposes of participation can identified:

a. Participation is inherently good.
b. It is a source of wisdom and information about local conditions, needs, and attitudes, and thus improves the effectiveness of decision-making.
c. It is an inclusive and pluralistic approach by which fundamental human needs are fulfilled and user values reflected.
d. It is a means of defending the interests of groups of people and of individuals, and a tool for satisfying their needs which are often ignored and dominated by large organizations, institutions, and their inflated bureaucracies.

Forms of participation

'Participation can be active or passive. A rough division of these two extremes results in opposing poles of expert autonomous and user autonomous architecture. The concept of expert autonomous architecture denotes architecture stemming from the architect's own, subjective ideas and values. Planning and design decisions are made by the architect, himself, alone, denying exposure to other opinions, i.e. 'artistic' architect. At the other end of the scale, in user autonomous architecture, the architect is more or less eliminated from the planning, design, and construction process' (Wulz, 1986). These two forms of architectural extremes may not appear very often today in their pure forms, but they do serve to illustrate the two opposing poles of the architectural design process. One where the architect reaches his own decisions and sets his personal stamp on his architecture, and the other, where the individual makes his own decisions and will not submit to anyone else's 'stamp' (Wulz, 1986). In the practical world of building, these two extremes are forced to reach a compromise with each other. The question is which one of the two is to make the decisive decisions in connection with the planning and design of the architectural environment. The different forms and stages of participation are a result of the differences of influence by the architect and the user. The scale between those two poles provide the stages of influence by the architect and by the user. It is a reciprocal scale where the decreasing influence of the architect is followed by increasing users influence.

In the following discussion, seven different forms and stages of participation are identified between the poles of expert autonomous architecture and user autonomous architecture as described by Wulz(1986). They are described as:

- representation
- questionnaires
- regionalism
- dialogue
- alternative
- co-decision
- self-decision

The most passive form of 'participation' is achieved by the architect's consideration for the user's desires and personal need. The architect's role is the interpreter of the explicit and the implicit desires, ambitions, dreams and self-esteem of the client. The client's influence on the architectural process and its result takes place by the architect's capability of putting himself in the place of the client. The user's influence in the process occurs through the architect, whose professional knowledge and experience permits him/her to assume the position of the unknown user with regard to their special needs. The architect represents the anonymous user through a personal and subjective interpretation of the user's situation.

Participation also occurs through the use of questionnaires in survey research studies. It consists of the statistical gathering of a user group's requirements. By this method an indirect form of participation of an annonymous group of people is achieved. The basis of indirect, or surrogate participation is the philosophy that what many people have in common is also preferred by the majority of the people that they represent. Variations, however, in people's attitudes and values has raised questions about this oversimplified and uniforming assumptions.

The reaction against the uniform residential areas of the 1960's with similar architectural appearance independent from their geographic and cultural situation, resulted in the demand to differentiate residential areas by putting them into a historical context. Conviction that the importance of specific regional and local characteristics for human well-being and a good environment led to the consideration of the characteristics of a local architecture. This approach entails inventorying the local population's preferences with regard to architectural expression, symbols, forms and spatial behavior. As distinct from questionnaries, regionalism considers the specific cultural heritage within a geographically limited area. The combination of 'representative thinking' with 'questioning' the local residents constitutes regionalism as a form of participation which directs itself towards the architectural and symbolic qualities in a specific area.

Dialogue or consultation is a form of participation that is most often based on informal conversations between the architect and the users who are encouraged to visit the architect and provide their personal input about the project. The dialogue model is based on the concept of using people's knowledge as a source of information and asking them to comment on the architect's proposal while the design process is in progress. This form of participation is based on two-way communication: information from the architect regarding his/her proposal, and at an early stage in the design process, comments and viewpoints from the users regarding the proposal. In this form of participation the architect reserves the right to make the final decisions.

Alternatives, is a form of participation that goes a step further in involving the user in the design process. It is based on a process whereby users are given the choice of several alternatives within a fixed set of boundaries. In order to facilitate choices, however, the alternatives have to be presented in a clear way for the lay person to understand. Visualization of an architectural proposal which reflects a future architectural environment is therefore fundamental for a meaningful participatory exchange of opinions. Alternative participation presupposes that the future user is known to the architect.

In all of the previously described forms of participation, it was the architect who had the decisive influence in the design process. In order to avoid any misunderstanding it should be added that the architect's decisions are often influenced by factors outside of the professional field. Co-decision as a method of participation, is mostly taking part in a balanced decision situation. Co-decision involves the population from the beginning of a design process, and aims at the user's direct and active participation.

Direct participation presupposes:

that the people involved are known,
that these individuals are interested in and motivated to participate,
that these individuals have time to be involved in all phases of the project;

If these conditions do not exist then there is a risk that co-decision as an active form will become more passive. In the self-decision context, the influence of the architect is reduced still further. The following two factors are decisive:

- people are seen as creative entities;

- people's independence from all forms of authoritative intervention is seen as the purest form of democracy.

These statements express two points of view that have in common the conception that people have a fundamental need and desire to express their own individuality and uniqueness as human beings. This approach may limit the number of people involved, since direct collaboration can be most effective within a small group. As an alternative to this limitation, the future users elect from among themselves representatives with the task of planning and decision making.

Representative planning is contrary to the principle of self-decision as the active direct participation of every individual. Self-decision participation is, in principle, just what participation is or should be all about, namely decision-making by the users themselves. Here, it is the task of the architect to ensure that society's fundamental demands of security are respected.

The structure of participation

The discussion about the forms of participation may have given the impression that it is the architect alone who takes initiative for the users taking part in the design process, or that it depends on him/her if demanded participation is rejected. The initiative can come from anyone affected by a design decision, in the same way that anyone invited to take part in a design process can decline. Participation is either requested from those who are to be effected by the changes in their architectural environment, or else they are offered participation by architects, or by the client.

It is also apparent that the interests of those involved in participation are related to different time periods in the participation process, which can be divided into three phases: (a) the design phase, (b) the construction phase, (c) and participation in administration and maintenance after the completion of the project. The effects of participation during those three phases can be the subject of considerable research. However, it can be assumed that involvement during different time periods can have considerable influence on the conditions for the design of buildings as well as of urban space (Hinrichs, 1985).

- Pre-programming involves users as soon as possible.
- Programming involves users in preparing and compiling the program.
- This stage is the most intense and time demanding for the user's representative as the most crucial of all stages for the user's organization.
- Preliminary design entails the review and search for alternatives.
- Design development involves the user by requiring additional detailed information.
- Working documents involves bidding and letting the contract.
- Construction involves occasional site meeting and reports.
- Post-occupancy evaluation involves users in reactions to the environment and a reassessment of the program and design decisions.

Levels of participation

As a convenient organizing system, a review of the literature will examine participation as a function of the type of structure in which it occurs. There are important qualitative differences in participation within small groups, and organizations; yet it is not always recognized that participation involves both levels.

Structural factors: Certain factors appear to influence both participant behavior and participation outcomes. These important structural factors include: group type, whether small face-to-face groups, formal organizations, or larger organizations of multiple groups; purpose of participation: degree of autonomy; participant characteristics; structural conduciveness; and resources available.

Behavior factors: In addition to structural factors, certain behavioral factors are also relevant to our view of participation. These include the information exchange process; participation outcome: whether the act succeeded or failed in terms of its goal; type and sequence of interaction: whether the interaction between participants was primarily coercive (conflict), utilitarian (competition), or normative (cooperation), and whether it changed over time; motivation: competence: capacity of participants to take effective roles in decision-making; and internal cohesiveness: extent to which group members are united behind leaders.

Small group participation

As a background to this theoretical discussion, general participation studies have been categorized in terms of whether the size of the unit of analysis was the small group, the organization, or the community. All of these different groups depend on the number of participants involved, the topic, and the social relationship.

Participation has been studied in small groups where each participant has the direct control over the innovation or strategy through intimate communication. In a review of the literature, Godschalk (1971), notes that small group participation occurs where members communicate on a face-to-face basis and are aware of each other as individuals. The small group studies produced evidence for the 'participation hypothesis,' as Verba (1961) states that: '...significant changes in human behavior can be brought about rapidly only if the persons who are expected to change participate in deciding what the change shall be and how it shall be made.'

The basis for the participation hypothesis stems from the nature of the influence of the small group over its individual members, causing them to conform to group standards, once these have been set. Thus conformity in one form or another is the typical dependent variable in small group studies. Conformity results from compliance with group norms, or rules, that describe expected behavior and prescribe punishments for noncompliance.

Small group members tend to conform to group norms because of individual needs (affective and opinion evaluation), internal pressures within the individual to be accepted by the group, and external pressures and sanctions imposed on the non-conformist by the group (Verba, 1961). The character of the small groups itself also affects the susceptibility of member opinions to group influence. Small groups tend to exert a great influence on member opinions because the member does not have the opportunity to be selective about the information he/she will be exposed to (unlike the mass media), relations among members are diffuse and general, rather than specific to any particular type of behavior, and informal decision methods emphasize consensus, unlike voting which allows for opinion differences (Verba, 1961). In the small group participation method the group leader acts as the medium between external enforcement and internal demands. Democratic (participatory) or authoritarian (coercive) decision methods may be applied, but in general, members have been found to prefer a democratic (normative) leadership style, and more readily accept decisions in which they have participated (Lewin, Lippitt, and White, 1939).

The 'participation effect' in small groups has been described in terms of a type of social physics. Norms supposedly set up a 'field of forces' acting on the group. Participation lowers the forces opposed to change, while external direction increases them and causes group tension and aggression. In this view the field of forces must appear to beinfluenced from within the group so that group and individual goals can be fused. For effective participation, members must make a positive commitment by actively discussing the subject. The force for decisions must come from the group, and members must perceive other members as changing (Verba, 1961). A major criticism of the early small group participation studies was that the structure did not offer alternatives for group decisions, but merely sought member endorsement of the leader's goals. The underlying analytical assumption appears as one of social control: individual conformity as the desired outcome where leadership was a means of changing group attitudes. Participation has also been linked to conflict behavior in small group studies based on game theory, where the underlying analytical assumption is one of exchange. Game theory assumes that it is possible to assign values to the various choices in conflicting issues, so that there is an explicitly, measurable basis for determining preferences. The game theory approach defines conflict as an exchange process based on competition or cooperation (Abt, 1970).

Organizational participation

Organizational theories of participation are most highly developed for large-scale, formal organizations in which members participate on a contractual basis under a model of inducements-contributions exchange. The participants in organizations generally tend to be members of voluntary organizations while the authorities tend to be employees of formal organizations. In voluntary organizations, where member participation is rewarded primarily with intangible social benefits, behavior is less regulated and predictable. The types of organizational participation are based on the concept of the 'prime beneficiary' as Blau and Scott (1962), identify four types of organizations:

Mutual benefit: in which the members are prime beneficiaries, and the mail problem is to maintain an internal democratic processes;

Business: in which the owners are prime beneficiaries, and attainment of maximum efficiency under competition is the main problem;
Service: in which the clients are prime beneficiaries, and conflict between administrative procedures and professional services are the main problem, and;
Commonwealth: in which the public at large is the prime beneficiary and development of democratic mechanisms for external public control is the main problem.

The main conflict within the organization may come from internal and/or external pressure. Both pressures can lead to change in organizational objectives and the search for innovation, however, the final solution is almost impossible to foresee.

Perhaps the major distinction between organization theorists is whether they assume organization equilibrium (achieved through rational strategies), of individual member development (achieved through cooperation) as their major goals. However, even those who see individual development by the normative means of human relations have been accused of harboring a social control perspective.

Participation as an organization strategy

Many of the social characteristics of society are integrally connected to the behavior of organizations and the delivery of goods and services. In organizational development, participation refers to an approach that is rooted in trust, intimacy, and consensus. This relationship has been described by William Ouchi (1981) as Theory Z, where Theory X is an assumption about human behavior (McGregor, 1960) which assumes that people are inherently lazy and need to be constantly watched; and Theory Y assumes that people are hard working and need only to be supported and encouraged. This distinction is significant since there is a growing number of Type Z organizations where the decision making process is typically a consensual, participative one. Egalitarianism is a central feature of Type Z organizations. Egalitarianism implies that each person can apply discretion and can work autonomously without close supervision, because they are to be trusted. This feature accounts for high levels of loyalty and productivity in Type Z organizations (Ouchi, p.81). Social scientists have described this as a democratic (as opposed to autocratic or apathetic) process in which many people are drawn into the shaping of important decisions. In Type Z companies, the decision making may be collective, but the ultimate responsibility for decisions still resides in one individual. The consensus process, as defined by Edgar Schein (1969), is one in which members of the group may be asked to accept responsibility for a decision that they do not prefer, but that the group, in an open and complete discussion, has settled upon. This combination of collective decision making with individual responsibility demands an atmosphere of trust. Through many years of research, Ouchi (1981), Likert (1967), and others have demonstrated that Type Z organizations were more profitable and had emotionally healthier employees than did the autocratic organizations.

This approach can serve to enhance the performance and experience of everyone involved in an organization. People do indeed gain satisfaction from feeling competent, in control, and free to choose for themselves. Personal involvement in the design of their workplace will aid the development of responsibility, cooperation, and self-motivation.

There has been a considerable amount of research pertaining to the study of organizations yet very little effort has gone into understanding the role of the physical setting or workplace. While organization theorists are sensitive to the social situations influencing work effectiveness, there is a lack of awareness of the impact of the environment upon work in organizations. Concern about productivity and worker motivation are basic to organizations as are rapid staff turnover, absenteeism and in some instances damage to or theft of plant facilities. This is explained by the early theorists' focus on formal and prescribed aspects of organizations with a concern for greater rationality and efficiency (Porter, Lawler & Hackman, 1975). Organizational problems which developed were usually attributed to 'recalcitrant workers.' Interest in the concept of work and the design of the workplace occupied in the time of industrial psychologists, operations researchers, and human factors specialists.

This is partially explained by the famous Hawthorne Studies in the late 1930's at Western Electric which explored how formal organizational factors and physical characteristics of the work environment, including varying light levels, influenced worker's performance. The results demonstrated the influence of the informal social structures which pervade organizations. People were subsequently viewed as operating within a social context such that the role of the workplace was isolated from the more pervasive social issues. The possibility that informal communication patterns, roles, norms and other social pressures were influenced by the workplace was not given much consideration.

Recently, however, some industrial organizations have adopted explicitly participative modes of decision making in which all members of a department or team reach consesus on what decisions to adopt. The concept of quality circles is an example which emerged in Japan during the early 1960's as an approach to improve the quality of their products. A basically volunteer concept, quality circles were formed by people who wanted to be in them. Once members had been trained in basic decision making concepts, the circle selected the workplace problems it wished to solve. While support staff such as facilitators and engineers provided guidance and technical information, the circle analyzed and solved the problems through their weekly meetings. The group could be said to have achieved consensus when it finally agreed upon a single alternative and each member of the group could honestly say to each other that there had been mutual understanding of all points of view, and, most importantly, that whether or not the group members preferred the decision, they would support it because it was arrived at in an open and fair manner.

Their solutions were presented to management who retained the final decision making authority concerning the appropriateness of the decision. The acceptance rate of circle ideas was usually high because of the detailed analysis and justification circle members provided when they presented a solution to management. The basic ingredient in this style of thinking was trust. From industry it has been learned that involved workers are the key to increased productivity. As a nation, the United States has developed a sense of the value of technology and a scientific approach to it, but meanwhile people have been taken for granted.

A recent review of worker productivity experiments suggest a series of trends associated with the application of behavioral analysis. Useful results were achieved in setting clear and difficult but attainable goals which typically involved prompt and frequent feedback. The wider sharing of responsibility and control, sometimes called participative management, is more than a philosophy - it usually is found to have positive results as well (Katzell, Bienstock & Forbstein, 1975). Any plan to improve or maintain productivity must be approached in terms of psychological, social, environmental and economic factors which must be integrated and harmonized if the system is to have long-term effectiveness.

A review of earlier literature summarizing the desires of people who work in industry suggests needs for self-direction or self-esteem and needs for affiliation and acceptance (Katz, 1960). Another observer of factors in motivation reports that 'when (workers) reported feeling happy with their jobs, they most frequently described factors related to their tasks... conversely, when feelings of unhappiness were reported they were not associated with the job itself but with conditions that surround the doing of the job' (Hertzberg, Mausner and Snyderman, 1959).

Another ingredient closely associated with the idea of participation is intimacy. Again, from industrial management it can be observed that the foremen who know their workers well can put together work teams of maximum effectiveness. Often bureaucratic rules of government or explicit procedures can cause productivity to decline. Furthermore, the idea of intimacy as a vital ingredient for a health society, has long been maintained by sociologists. In the American mind, however, it is believed that intimacy should be supplied from certain sources. The church, the family and other traditional institutions are the only legitimate sources of intimacy. There has been resistance to the idea that there can or should be close familiarity with people in the workplace. Personal feelings have no place at work, is the common belief.

This theory and approach opens the way for people to find and pursue points of communality involving their own interests and those of the organizations for which they work. This approach can also serve to enhance the performance and experience of everyone involved in an organization. Considering that the basic idea is to replace an adversary relationship, as is typically produced by theory and management, with a cooperative, problem solving approach, it makes good sense that beneficial results should follow. People do indeed gain satisfaction from feeling competent, in control, and free to choose for themselves. Personal involvement in the design of their workplace will aid the development of responsibility, cooperation, and self-motivation.

The design of workplaces, and the proper matching of the capabilities of workers and machines are widely considered to be solved problems. It is generally believed that further productivity gains will probably come from the organizational aspects of production. Production and quality standards usually establish acceptable levels and quality of output. When these measures show below standard performance, they signal that something is wrong with the workplace, but not what the problem is. Generally, the method used to solve the problem is for management to request that the industrial engineer, production manager or quality control engineer study the situation and propose solutions. Another method is to ask the workers what the problem is, since they are a resource that is not fully utilized in many organizations. Management, though, may often assume that workers are not knowledgeable about what the problems are and how to solve them. There is ample evidence, however, that workers can and will contribute to problem identification as well as the solution.

In a study of a plant experiencing quality problems, one hundred people were interviewed while they were working (Hancock and Walton, 1977). They were told that in a properly designed workplace they should have the necessary information, materials, tools and machines to do their job. Of the 100 employees, 75 responded that their workplaces were deficient in at least one of these regards. The most frequent problems were: tooling in poor repair, input parts not to specifications, improper training and lack of information. Many of the workers also appeared to be upset by the problems of their workplace. They were feeling hasseled because the organization did not maintain their workplaces. When asked if they told their foreman about the problems they were having, many responded that they had, but that the foreman was not able to remedy the situation. Previous investigations had concluded that the workers were simply 'no good,' were 'lazy' and had 'poor attitudes.'

There have been numerous studies in the production facility of automotive plants, engineering units in public utilities where it has been found that there is a close connection between workers' attitudes and the mechanistic aspects of the workplace. If workers are unable to perform, others perceive that they have to work unnecessarily hard to accomplish their tasks, and if managment does not respond to requests for improvement, poor attitudes are likely to result.

Quality is one of the important indicators of the proper functioning of the mechanistic aspects of the workplace. When workers are informed about how their workplaces should be, they are useful detectors concerning workplace problems. Druker (1968), summarizes ways to reach the goal of a responsible worker as providing the worker with information needed for self control and opportunities for participation that will offer a managerial vision. While others look at participation as a form of participants involved in the process, in the Burke perspective, participation is a 'strategy for attaining organizational goals,' stressing its social control aspects in four of his five strategies. The five strategies outlined by Burke (1968) include:

1. Education therapy in which individuals working together learn how a democracy works and how to cooperate in problems, as well as developing self-confidence;
2. Behavioral change in which the objective is to change the behavior of the members of the system by changing group norms and by encouraging group members to take part in the decision-making process;
3. Staff supplement in which citizens are recruited to carry out organization tasks for which staff resources are lacking;

4. Cooperation in which citizens or representatives of groups are involved in an organization in order to avert threats to the organization;
5. Community power in which an organization selects conflict or confrontation techniques to gain participation in decision-making within an established power structure.

In the first four strategies, the direction of participation is downward from the organization to the citizens, who are used in various ways to achieve organizational ends. In the fifth strategy, the target is not the form of participation in intra-organization, but inter-organizational. From an organizational viewpoint, trying to put participation within a planning perspective is recognized (as the difficulty of actively involving participants) in the heart of the planning process--the working through of the problem. Participants have their own specific expertise, values, and knowledge. According to the participatory method, people design and plan for themselves and may not necessarily share the values of the other participants in the group. This causes conflicts and arguments, unless there is a common understanding of the framework to resolve the arguments (Godschalk, 1972).

From the organizational development viewpoint, most approaches used in achieving employee effectiveness and satisfaction have largely been directed towards people and the work process. The work environment has been treated as a residual after people and processes. The physical environment, when conceived and managed as an active resource supporting people and work processes, can become a part of the organization's development process. People, processes, and the workplace, have been separated in an organizational chart, yet this interaction needs to be seen as a single entity if people's performance is to be considered.

If the physical environment can be envisioned as a tool for organizational renewal, then there needs to be a developmental process where the facility does not end at the finished construction of a building. Rather, there needs to be an ongoing development of the workplace environment that matches the organizational changes as they occur. Facilities require managing, which is long range in commitment, and enables participation at all organizational levels in problem solving and decision making. The results will increase the effectiveness of the organization through the increased involvement of people in their work. Organizations, however, will need to understand the workplace as a dynamic entity and subsequently seek new means for this transformation. More experimentation in the workplace coupled with demonstration projects can provide the substantive information base that is necessary to encourage new attitudes to emerge. Monitoring the workflow process and workplace appropriateness through observation, surveys, and interviews will enable workers and management groups to participate in achieving a dynamic balance between human factors and the workplace.

Community participation

Community participation is the larger scale planning process which provides the trends for small group and organizations to follow. The changes and conflicts involve more complex processes than that of small group and organzational participation. Usually the changes are directed towards controlled community actions which are difficult to control. As Warren (1965) nas noted: '...most purposive social change at the community level is of a secondary, rather than a basic nature, being a response to the uncontrolled aggregate of decisions to do one thing or another by individual actors in the community, or a response to the behavior of various adaptive organizations which have been set up to cope with these basic changes, or a response to changes occuring in the unity as part of a national trend and not separable from it.'

Participation in community level planning and governance defies the simpler analytic approaches used for small groups and organizations, although it occurs in these settings as well as others, particularly in the inter-organizational context. Innovation and conflict at the community level are more complex processes, where the checks and balances of political systems tend to temper outcomes and where changes often occur as a reaction to forces beyond community control. Political processes have played the most rapid change in decision - making. The changes have been described by Godschalk (1972) that: '...political processes are often used to explain the conservative nature of communities. In a democracy, citizens replace their government leaders periodically, unlike employees or clients of an organization. The continuous threat of losing an election is a powerful counterforce against the introduction of social change by government, and is often used to explain why a crisis is necessary to justify radical changes in public programs.'

Working with groups

A participatory process developed by Halprin and Burns described in their book *Taking Part: AWorkshop Approach to Collective Creativity* (1974), was the focus of the design of a Catholic Secondary School in Berkeley, California. Their process entails involving the people who will use the project in a series of participatory workshops at the very outset of conceptual planning. For 10 years the students, faculty, parents, administrators and neighbors of St. Mary's College High School have been working together to determine changes in the environment of the 12 acre campus. The results that have emerged include a brother's residence, a student center, a central plaza and site planning.

At the initial workshop in 1974, students, teachers, administrators, parents and community people began their planning process by exploring the physical and non-physical qualities of St. Mary's. First, they were asked to prepare 'real life' plans for the campus on scaled base maps. With the help of a professional team, people prepared their plans to demonstrate their recommendations for the campus. The plans were then presented for discussion and commented on and the workshop conductors offered a summary of the agreements and differences that emerged. The workshop had taken one full

Saturday and more than 80 people participated. When the campus plan was developed, workshop representatives reviewed it to insure that it reflected the agreements that were previously reached. Soon after, actual work began on several projects.

In 1981, Marquis Associates and Burns (1983) returned to St. Mary's to involve people in updating and changing the campus plan according to newly stated needs. The professional team re-involved people in the wide range of campus planning issues, changing previous decisions, and making new decisions with the aid of a take-apart scale model of the campus. Commenting on user-participation as an aid to professional programming, Marquis' associate partner, Caldwell, states that 'workshops quickly gave us information for which we otherwise would have worked for weeks, and some of it we would never never discovered, buried as it was in people's personal feelings' (1983).

Architects Lewis and Gindroz (1974) describe their participatory experiences in the design of a human resource center in Pontiac, Michigan as one that deeply influenced their mode of subsequent practice. In the course of a complex and open process involving a great many people, sometimes in bitter confrontation, sometimes in quiet working sessions, a building form emerged that included learning areas for children and adults, a health center, theaters and a library, a community field house, a good co-op, workshops and studios, food service for the elderly and a public restaurant and lounge. What they learned there, and have since seen repeated in a number of situations, is that when consumers and citizens are openly enfranchised early in the design process and invited to assume creative and responsible roles, planners and architects suddenly find available to them undreamed of resources of local perceptions and wisdom and the reinforcement of the community.

Roadblocks to participation

Since the ideas associated with participation are new to the design field, there are detractors, skeptics and a more general body of professionals who regard this as a passing fad. As a result, there are numerous arguments against participation, some of which are valid while others are simply false assumptions. The most persistent argument against participation is the proposition that teams cannot design; that design is an individual activity.

The camel is facetiously cited as a horse designed by a team or committee. The emphasis, however, on individual genius has been over romanticized by designers who report the creative act in terms of inexplicable insight, neglecting the daily routine that has given the insight an underpinning. Decision making by consensus has been the subject of considerable research and the evidence strongly suggests that a consensus approach yields more creative decisions and more effective implementation that does individual decision making (Schein, 1969).

Overemphasis on the group as an ultimate creative context can be equally detrimental whether the group is called a team, a task force or a committee. Quite often, groups without a disciplined approach degenerate towards the level of the safest or the most obvious solution. The thinking which underlies most naive group activity is that the capabilities of the participants are additive; that three moderately creative individuals are equal to one highly creative individual. Similarly, another mistaken belief is that if one member does not think of a solution, another may. If none arrive at a solution, then the blame is equally spread throughout the group.

Many of these problems can be resolved practically if every member of the group is personally committed to solving the problem in the best possible way so that participants can shift their emphasis from personal capabilities to collective capabilities. A willingness to openly recognize better solutions is the key ingredient for group success. Similarly, effective groups would need to shape the collective expertise of each of the members. Psychologist Gordon, author of Synectics, (1961) describes a process aimed at the development of creative capacity, and substantiates the idea that the individual process in the creative act enjoys a direct analogy in group process.

Since groups attempt to expand the expertise of the individual, then it is necessary to consider the limitations of the experts whether they represent the user population, the client, government or other designers. Quite frequently complaints result from experiences with user groups or committees, people's wants are rooted in their experience, that many groups' aspirations are common-place and mundane, that the designer's responsibility is to expand the horizons of the group. Since these observations are certainly valid, it may be useful to clarify these beliefs.

The quality of expertness consists of access to special knowledge of a subject which supposedly raises the individual's awareness above that which is obvious. In reality, the expert is the least able to create a new idea since the problem is often described in the technical terms of the expert's language so that it is impossible to view the problem in a new way. Yet the knowledge of the expert is necessary to state the obvious or the commonplace in order to expand the narrowness of vision often found in highly trained people. Sometimes an attack on convention is viewed as an attack on the people themselves and results in experts who do not function as individuals but as images of themselves. Communication is necessary at the personal as well as the professional level if there is any expectation for group activity to achieve more than the obvious.

Another issue frequently cited refers to people's residential and job mobility. Since the time span for the renovation or construction of a new building through occupancy may take several years, opponents of participation have argued that the original participants may have or will soon leave, thus invalidating their involvement in the design process. For many years this recurring myth has plagued designers: the design tailored to the departing individual--whether resident or employee--will have to be redone. That there have been similar proclamations about residential recreation projects as well as student housing, suggests that since there are individual differences among people, the best way to cope with this situation is to ignore individual differences and design for no one in particular. Quiet often building programs do not always produce an accurate assessment of existing facilities in terms of people's use, preferences, or complaints. Lacking such information, the program usually relies on an idealized stereotype about the building's occupants. Institutional clients rely on building committees to advocate the user's point of view. Such committees are often far removed from the needs of those who actively use the building.

Since people have such different needs, attempts to create a single standardized 'ideal' environment works to everyone's disadvantage. However, simply creating physical variety does not solve the problem. The user must participate in this process as an agent to assure variety. Consequently, designers can create places that encourage individual choice in spite of situations that involve high occupancy turnover. People's desire for personal territory, privacy, flexibility, and appropriateness are all design concerns that are often difficult to measure directly in relation to the institutional balance sheet. Often it is the user and his/her community who pay the psychic and social consequences of ill-fitting environments.

Organizing a participatory event

Participation in design and planning has come to be construed as an acceptable concept. However, in most instances serious demands and responsibilities are placed upon participants. Where economic constraints are severe enough to exclude design assistance, citizen groups may voluntarily organize themselves for action. Although social and church groups as well as professional societies have assumed an orientation towards accomplishing social goals and do participate in community projects, the technical complexity of creating new or rehabilitating existing housing usually requires substantial design assistance. In addition to concern with technical complexity, sound design principles must also be incorporated in the development process. Without guidance, community groups may respond only to crisis situations and subsequently cannot achieve the broad goals that originally united the group. Often community volunteers cannot draw upon personal experiences for resolving environmental conflicts and may select courses of action that create unforseen, delecterious consequences. Therefore, the management of participatory efforts directed at environmental change is important.

People will join together if it is clear that change can and will occur. Participation can function if it is active, directed, and a sense of achievement is experienced by those who get involved. At the same time, it requires a re-examination of traditional design procedures to insure that participation becomes more than affirmation of the designer's intentions. The guidance of citizen participation directed at environmental change requires new skills of the design professional, both design skills and skills for ensuring community participation in the design process.

Structuring group efforts can take many forms corresponding to the variety of environmental issues that confront communities daily. The basic ingredient in the participatory process is individual learning through awareness of a problem. Learning occurs best when the process is clear, communicable, open, and encourages dialogue, debate, and collaboration. As more people learn about environmental issues and impacts, the decisions they make will have broad effects on the quality of the environment.

Thus, the designer's role is to facilitate the user group's ability to reach decisions pertinent to the environment through a communicable procedure. Most often this will take the form of creating awareness which permits citizens to be critical of environmental alternatives. Such design assistance is oriented toward sensitizing groups to environmental issues.

The facilitator's role is to help people develop their resources in ways that will benefit themselves and others. Facilitation helps bring people together to determine what they wish to do and helps them find ways to work together in figuring out ways to do it. A facilitator's role is to make everyone know that they are included in what is going on and that what they have to say is being listened to by the group. Facilitation can also include systematic procedures by which non-design trained people can organize themselves to create a planned action. The basic ingredient in the participatory process is individual learning through increased awareness of a problem. Learning occurs best when the process is clear, communicable, and open, and encourages dialogue, debate and collaboration.

If people are to discover the principle of quality for themselves, they are more likely to do so in small groups. But, above and beyond this, small-scale organization is needed to reduce alienation and to allow people to come to grips with rapid change. Significant changes in human behavior can be brought about rapidly only if the persons who are expected to change participate in deciding what the change shall be and how it shall be made. Participation, however, can take place through many modes of involvement including simulated experiences and structured group decision making.

Simulation methods are primarily educational since their purpose is to prepare people to act. Such methods are based on an abstraction of complex processes achieved by compressing time and capturing the interest of participants through 'parlor game' strategies. Gaming simulations devised by architects ask participants to assume the decision roles normally included in 'real life' situations. It is hoped that after participation in a game process, individuals will confront their own community problems with an increased awareness of the general issues, the process by which decisions are made, and appropriate decision strategies. This approach is utilized to make individuals more sensitive to issues and alternatives, and ultimately to influence individual behavior.

Another form of participation is the direct involvement of community residents in a systematically organized decision process. This process can be professionally designed for a specific community issue or a general planning process can be utilized for typical classes of problems. Success in this approach is associated with the quality of guidance through the decision procedure. Leadership is necessary to insure that all the participants contribute to the fullest of their abilities. Similarly, the procedures are tailored to the willingness of people who are required to work together, yet are not intended to force involvement beyond a participant's competence. Overzealous attempts at total involvement of community residents in all stages of the design process may lead to early withdrawl, particularly if progress toward implementation is slow. An effective process for involving people must be carefully designed. The random involvement of people without a clear sequence of events and without clearly understood roles can result in chaos. There are a few essential ingredients for success in any type of participatory effort. Initially there needs to be a shared view of the goals of the project and what the participants want to achieve. As the process moves ahead the goals may change, yet the structure should be adhered to since open-ended processes that permit people to join and drop out usually end in frustration. To insure continuity of the process, a steering committee, executive board, citizens council, or building committee should be formed at the outset. Their role should also include the need to maintain open communication between all participants at all times. Open dialogues often provide protection against hidden agendas that may emerge. It is also quite important for the process to have a clear beginning and end where participants understand their responsibilites and how they are interconnected with each other and with the designer. The role of the designer in this process is not only as the process facilitator, but as the technical specialist who makes recommendations and develops the necessary design documents. Since the process is open to lay people, communication systems which everyone can read clearly must be employed.

Organizing the workshop

The term 'workshop' is used to emphasize that participants engage in those experiences that provide the material for learning about human relations. The assumption is that learning is most functional when it grows out of personally involving experiences that require reflecting, developing and testing of new insights and approaches to problem solving. These processes come into focus when participants are obliged to resolve their differences in pursuit of a common goal.

Workshops are an appropriate setting to achieve a high level of interaction between people sharing a common purpose. A workshop is a planned event whereby participants can learn from each other as they explore issues. An important component in the development of a workshop is that of building cohesion. Opportunities should be provided for groups to get so involved with each other that they begin to see each other as persons and, therefore, invest interest in each other. It is the intent of this experience to facilitate learning that might otherwise be haphazard and diffuse. In order to accomplish this, it is necessary to structure the experience to insure that there is a focus to the group process. It should also increase the probability that certain learning will occur for the participants. The structured experience, however, does not dictate what a participant should learn.

The structured experience is a function of the objectives of the experience, the content, and the techniques employed to focus learning. The learning goals of a structured experience may include cognitive, affective and skill building aspects. The cognitive aspect of the experience may include an awareness of the content or uses and how they can be effectively organized. The participant's self awareness, insight and empathy illustrate the affective aspects of learning goals. Development and implementation of characteristics such as listening and problem solving are skill building aspects of the goals. The content areas refer to individual and group events. They include methods of interpersonal communication, group problem solving, sensory awareness, giving and receiving feedback, and team building. Techniques employed to direct learning include activities such as making or building something, discussions, summarizations, board games, interviews, inventories or check lists, role playing, and tasks.

An appropriate combination of objectives and techniques will produce a structure that will generate an opportunity for learning. Workshops can vary widely in topics, time lengths and goals, so it is necessary that all three be carefully chosen. The content and quality of the experience is important enough to create the highest quality environment possible. Since the workshop participants will be using various awareness activities to heighten their sensitivity to the environment, the meeting space and graphic quality are important factors that may contribute towards a successful session. The quality of meeting space should reflect an awareness of the environment by insuring adequate ventilation and light, movable furniture and a general setting that would make the participants feel comfortable. Arrangements setting the audience apart from the speaker are not desirable since it is important to establish a feeling of informality and encourage interaction.

Generally it is useful to promote an upcoming workshop, especially those open to the public, with mail flyers, press releases to the newspaper, and television and radio coverage. Participants attending workshops should receive an information packet including the program and workshop schedule. It is also useful to document the workshop by taking photographs, slides, video tapes, or audio cassettes, as well as recording the decisions that were made.

Certain activities are basic to any environmental workshop. First, it is necessary to clearly state the workshop's goals, schedule and events. Participants will become involved if they know what to expect. As an opening activity it is desirable to provide the participants with the opportunity to have a tangible personal experience that will relate to what they will encounter. This overview might take the form of a simple lecture, the presentation of environmental issues, or a slide show, which introduces basic concepts of awareness, understanding and action. The focus should be on active participation in activities that involve all the senses, allowing discovery and encouraging exploration. Each participant should carry from the workshop new information and fresh insights.

When individuals come together to engage in group tasks, perceptions of why the group was formed will effect their performance. It is important that there be a leader who will clarify the members roles and group objectives of the workshop. Appropriate role definitions will help reduce status barriers among members, encourage free communication, and decrease the tendency for high-status individuals to be unduly verbal. Workshop participants need to understand the context of their discussions and see the potential of their collective creativity before the process starts. Workshop participants should be divided into groups of five to nine people, since groups of fewer than five people may lack the knowledge or critical judgements available to analyze the problem and arrive at a decision. As groups enlarge beyond nine people, opportunities to participate decline and dissatisfaction occurs. A group leader or facilitator is needed to help members share activities and learn to work together.

Antagonism and conflicts arise when groups create together just as they do in 'real-life' situations. In both situations negative and destructive forces can emerge which can destroy personal relationships and group cohesiveness, or they can be used as positive forces for dynamic change and interchange. The core of the issue is to recognize conflict and to make it acceptable and visible, not attempt to squelch it or deny its validity. Conflict, when looked upon as an important resource, can become useful rather than destructive.

One major source of conflict in community workshops occurs when participants feel that their viewpoints are not being heard and, for this reason, they become belligerent and antagonistic. It is the responsibility of the group facilitator to see that conflicts, when they arise, are settled amicably and constructively. One of the important ways of resolving conflicts is for the leader to listen to what is said and then to repeat it - making sure of what the person or the group has said. This is called the language of acceptance, which means that one person accepts the other person for what he/she is and how he/she feels, even though you may not agree with him. A recorder working with each group is also an important contributor to the successful operation of the process. The recorder's function is to keep notes about what everyone in the group says so that in feedback sessions, each person has the assurance that he or she is being listened to and their input is being valued. Summaries is one method of group feedback which helps to resolve conflicts. After each session, the group leader can summarize the important points that were made insuring that everyone's point of view has been accurately stated. This insures that the process evolves on a basis of common agreements and people can identify and accept accomplishments before proceeding to the next activity.

In participatory sessions, opinions, biases and judgements have their place, but their purpose is to allow choice and encourage imput rather than to prevent ideas from flowing. Summaries during the session allow the group to perceive what has been happening and to determine how to proceed. Agreements can be reached or disagreements can be made visible so they can be constructively resolved.

Concurrently, with the exploration of people's perceptions of the issues, designers and planners need to develop a thorough data base in order to understand the technical aspects of the problem and synthesize them into issues, objectives and activities. Finally, this information is diagrammed in a series of easily understood drawings and models. Based on the objectives that were agreed upon in the workshops, a series of program alternatives can be developed in diagrammatic design form. These are discussed in meetings with appropriate groups and may be presented to the larger community for approval. The intention is to arrive at a consensus as to which of the design solutions best respond to the concerns of all participants. This final public forum, workshop or design is a necessary step prior to implementation of the project.

Conclusion

Participation might be seen as direct public involvement in decision making processes. In this type of participation, citizens share in decisions that determine the quality and direction of their lives. This requires the provision of effective communication media in order to provide suitable grounds for citizen participation in designing. The experiences in design participation show that the main source of user satisfaction is not so much the degree to which his/her needs have been met but the feeling of having influenced the decisions. However, there are many benefits accruing from such an approach for community, users and designers (Wrona, 1981).

Firstly, from the social point of view:

- it results in a greater meeting of social needs and an increasingly effective utilization of resources at the disposal of a particular community;
- it enhances democracy in the whole investment system;
- it has a didactic effect leading to increased social awareness and a generally higher intellectual level of community.

Secondly, to the user group in design:

- an increased reconciliation of his objectives;
- an increased sense of having influenced the design decision-making process;
- an increased awareness of the consequences of decisions made.

Thirdly, to the designer:

- setting up a logical basis for interdisciplinary design ventures operating through a mutual complement of professionals and non-professionals rather than through a domination of one group over the other;
- supplying the designer with more relevant and up-to-date information than was possible before;
- creating a methodological framework for an effective use of rational design methods and accurate design tools, such as the computer, without affecting the role and nature of creative processes now augmented by lay productions;
- enriching professional designers with non-professional aspects of social activity;
- expanding the role of professional designers to include the function of instructor and designer of the design process which admittedly burden them with new duties and responsibilities, but at he same time increase their social standing, esteem and respect.

The potential benefits offered by an organized approach to design participation constitutes logical, emotional, technological, and economic tenets for its use.

A collective review of the theories and practices of participation can be summarized as follows:

- The designer's job is no longer to produce finished and unalterable solutions, but to extract solutions from a continuous dialogue with those who will use his/her work. The designer's energy and imagination will be completely directed to raising the level of awareness of client/users in the discussion, and the solution will come out of the exchanges between two; the designer states opinions, provides technical information, and discusses consequences of various alternatives, just as the users state their opinions and contribute their expertise.
- Participation has a diversity of expression. A design and planning task resulting from this approach should be made 'transparent' in order for the final decisions to be understood by the people who will be effected by them.

•Public forums should be convened, and participation by all members of the community should be encouraged. In this way people can openly express their opinions, make necessary compromises, and arrive at acceptable decisions. This method not only strengthens the product by the wealth of input, but the user group is strengthened as well by learning more about itself.

•Although participation in the design process can create technological specialization by bringing numerous specialists in various fields to cooperate in design, a general effort should be made to educate the public about planning matters to achieve effective and efficient participation in designing.

•Public comments and representation should be accepted into the planning process continuously. The final decision is not the end of the process. It must be managed, evaluated and adapted to changing needs. Architecture in the future should be characterized by an increasing participation of the user in its organizational and formal definition. In order to respond to this situation, professionals will need to do everything possible to make design solutions less representative of its designers and more representation of its users, even though many difficulties in applying design participation arise as a result of organizational and methodological problems.

Participatory design of a branch library : A case study

This case study describes how citizen input was incorporated into the design of a 4600 square foot branch library located in Santa Cruz County, California. Emphasis is placed on planning the participation process and citizen consultation techniques. This project illustrates how consultation with local people helped create the library's site plan, floor plan arrangement, building form, and many of the significant architectural features of the library. Furthermore, it is the intent of this case study to stress that the process of being involved in the design, as well as the acceptability of the design,were benefits of the participation process. Jeff Oberdorfer, Architect, planned and facilitated the community participation process.

The planning process for the Boulder Creek Branch Library was triggered by two unrelated events. First, the nationally publicized flooding and destruction near Boulder Creek, several years earlier, focused community attention on the need for a self sufficient community center and meeting place. Bolder Creek is a rural area and during an emergency, the community can be isolated from the services provided in the nearby city of Santa Cruz. Second, a library site was donated in the downtown Boulder Creek vicinity, within walking distance of much of the community.

The County of Santa Cruz released a Request for Proposals (RFP) inviting architectural services for the design of the Boulder Creek Branch Library. Two important features of the RFP were:

- 'the design should provide for the maximum energy efficiency including the use of natural light and the application of passive solar design'
- 'the selected architect shall conduct a community participation process to ensure responsiveness to the needs and desires of the community.'

The RFP also included standards related to the size of the facility, the required functional spaces, handicapped accessibility, shelving capacity, parking requirements, and the size of population to be served.

A specially designated City/County Library Advisory Committee selected the architectural firms of van der Ryn/Calthorpe and Jeff Oberdorfer to collaborate on the design of the library. The selection of Oberdorfer was based on his demonstrated commitment to citizen participation, and van der Ryn/ Calthorpe for their pioneering work in energy conserving design.

Prior to the development of the participation process, the design and building constraints were identified. They included components of the RFP, as well as the site constraints, such as slope, location of significant redwood trees, solar orientation, and other possible factors that might limit site planning options.

The focus for community participation included the following issues:

- the location and arrangement of spaces within the library
- site plan relationships, such as slope, building orientation, user entry and arrival, parking location, and the character of exterior spaces
- the feeling, or ambience, of the library and surrounding site .

A graphic 'hands-on' approach is the primary method of user participation advocated by Oberdorfer, where small working groups of 5 to 7 people are engaged in a process of consensus decision making (Sanoff, 1978). The working groups were supplied all the materials they required, and were asked that they reached consensus for all decisions developed collaboratively. Progress reports were made periodically to the entire workshop group, allowing for comparisons between small groups. The participatory process was structured into three workshops that focused on the following issues:

Workshop 1: establish goals for the library
record or illustrate 'patterns' that describe the 'feeling' the library should evoke

Workshop 2: develop preliminary site plan drawings
develop preliminary floor plan drawings

Workshop 3: select the most appropriate floor plan/site plan options for final development by the architect

Workshop 1

The purpose of this session was to identify the goals for the library. This was conceived of as a large group meeting, with one member of the consulting team facilitatating the discussion, and another recording participant's comments on large sheets of paper mounted on the wall. In order to ensure a free flow of ideas, and to prevent participants from being intimidated by others, the goals discussed were not evaluated, even when some appeared contradictory. This brainstorming session generated 43 goals for the new Library. A summary of the goals are as follows:

'The Library should invite and be accessible to children.'
'The Library should accommodate teenage social activities, but these should be acoustically screened from other areas.'
'Provide visually attended space for youngsters who are dropped off at the Library after school in lieu of childcare.'
'Create a strong interrelationship between inside and outside; provide tall windows so we can see the trees.'
'The Library building itself should be a learning experience; energy eficient features shall be visible learning experiences in themselves.'
'Provide outdoor music, theater, performance areas and facilities.'
'The Library should be a model for future buildings in Boulder Creek, while being enduring enough so that we have something to pass on to future generations.'
'The Library should have a large, open entry-inviting to everyone.'
'Consider the Library a Community Center.'
'The Library should be a home for the local arts, both on display as well as integrated into the building.'
'Save on-site redwoods, palm trees, and existing fruit trees.'

'Generate 'real giving' from the Community in terms of the arts, sweat equity, and volunteerism, and incorporate into the building.'
'Develop a courtyard with varying level changes.'
'The Library should provide a 'stand by' Center in case of Community emergencies.'
'The Library should be a home away from home and always be open.'

During the second session of the workshop, participants were organized into small groups and asked to write or illustrate 'concepts' or 'patterns' they perceived as key features of a successful Library. The idea of patterns was based on Alexander's (1977) use of the term, however, they were conceived of, and generated by the participants (Figure 3.1). Oberdorfer suggests that 'the learning and creative experience developing patterns is quite different from the learning experience generated by choosing patterns from a book. This is an extremely important point in relationship to the empowerment that participants experience from the act of *participating*.'

When this phase of the workshop was completed participants discussed all the ideas developed in a free and non-critical exchange. Approximately 30 patterns were drawn or described, some of which are shown below:

- Provide a mudroom/changing area adjacent to the entry.
- Provide private read/study carrols as well as window seats in Bay Windows.
- Provide a variety of spaces in terms of size and height.
- Activities should fan out from the circulation desk in a circular manner.
- Windows should have lots of lites 'so it feels good' and should be set back deep to soften the light.
- Columns should do things and not just provide structural support.
- Steps should be designed so that we can sit on them for reading and conversation.
- The Library shall have a big front door to invite everyone in.
- Provide clerestories and natural light from above.
- 'Show off our wood,'consider using donated local woods for beams, etc.
- Consider loft spaces for kids, with shoe storage below, use lots of pillows in the kids areas.

Workshop 2

This workshop began with a summary of the preceding meeting for people attending for the first time. The main agenda was the development of the entire site. Participants were divided into eight working groups and asked to develop a consensus plan considering the following factors:

- location of the library on the site
- location of access roads and parking
- pedestrian paths and library entry
- specific concerns raised by neighbors (such as noise, litter, and a teenage hangout)

Figure 3.1 Patterns: 'steps that you can sit on' and 'a big front door'

Participants were expected to freely express ideas using sketch plans. By encouraging consensus decision-making, each group made trade-offs in order to reach a viable solution. Figure 3.2 is an example of a site plan developed by one work group. Here, as in other plans, solar orientation and daylight were important features. While collating the ideas from each group's design solutions, it became clear to Oberdorfer, that one plan could accommodate the community's wishes. The similar features of the participants' plans included:

- entryways on the east side
- solar access considerations, outdoor decks, and reading rooms on the south side
- parking on the east side
- minimal activity and development of the west side
- the utilization of existing heritage redwood trees on the south of the building to frame outdoor spaces

The similarity of the plans developed by the participants suggested that one rather than several options would be presented at the third workshop. The Library Advisory Committee agreed with this direction, and participants were notified by mail about the change in direction, and included in the mailing was a conceptual plan of the proposed Library design (Figure 3.3).

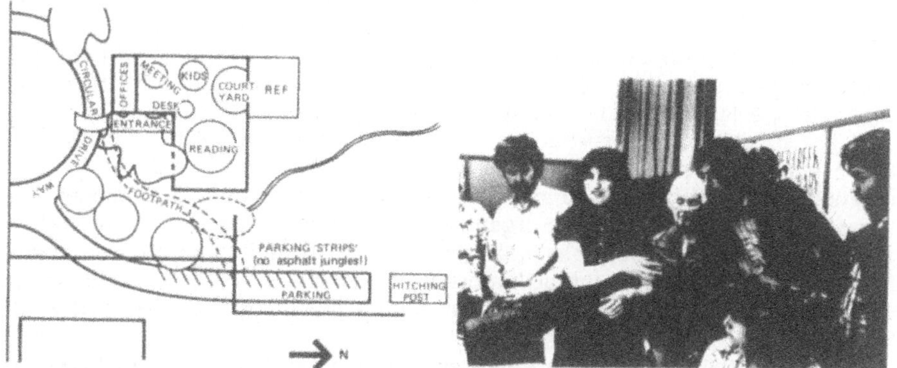

Figure 3.2 Consensus group site plan, and groups discussing drawings

Workshop 3

This final meeting was attended by 55 enthusiastic members of the community. It began with a slide show, presented by the architects, of the library building on the site, and illustrated how the patterns developed by the participants in Workshop 1 had been integrated into the design. Only one pattern strongly supported by the community was unable to be incorporated into the design. The pattern identified a loft space where children could read and play. However, because such a space would be inaccessible to a wheelchair, it was not included in the proposal. A scale model of the design solution was presented and warmly received by the community. The enthusiasm generated by the participatory process continued through the public hearing process and after construction.

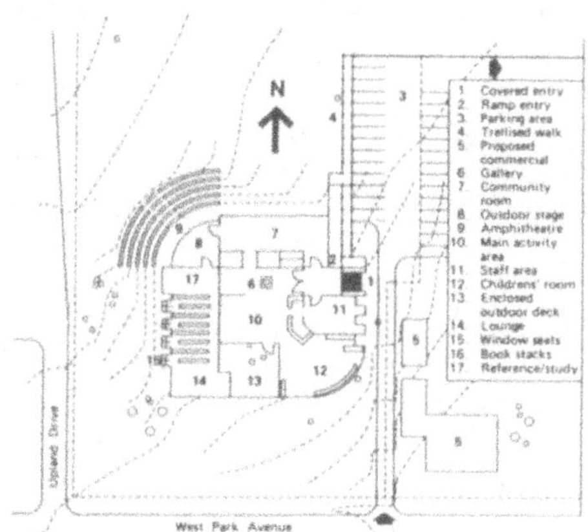

Figure 3.3 Concept plan of the library presented to participants at workshop 3

Conclusion

The participatory approach developed for the Boulder Creek Branch Library was based on a profile of the community and their needs; a detailed building program provided by the Library Advisory Committee; and the site constraints, solar access, and location of heritage redwood trees.

The success of the process is due to the determination of the community to create an independent building, symbolic of the community's desire for self reliance, and a willingness to make the necessary compromises to make the library a reality. Similarly, the organizational structure based on small work groups, diffused the possible intimidation often found in public hearings. Most of all, the architect and facilitators were perceived as allies, sharing their skills and expertise with that of the community members, thus de-mystifying the design process.

In June 1987, the Boulder Creek Branch Library won a national design award from the American Institute of Architects (AIA). The Library was among six libraries selected from over 135 entries throughout the United States (Figure 3.4).

Acknowledgment

This case study is summarized from an article by Jeff Oberdorfer, 'Community participation in the design of the Boulder Creek Branch Library,' that appeared in *Design Studies* (1988) 9.1:4-13, Guest Editor: Henry Sanoff.

Figure 3.4 Library viewed from the east, illustrating entryway

4 Applying theory Z principles

An integrated process

The integration of design research and participation is proposed as a new paradigm for effectively utilizing the knowledge that is generated by the environment-behavior research community. This is an outgrowth of traditional research approaches that are not capable of dealing with goals, values, and problem solving (Weisman,1983). Similarly, the behavioral research model, which consists of an institutionalized separation of research and application does not facilitate collaboration among researchers and designers (Seidel, 1982). This new notion stems from Lewin's (1946) concept of action research, a model that not only integrates theory and practice, but requires that one must act on a system in order to understand it, and that the designer/researcher will consequently have some effect on the outcome. The model consists of a series of cylical steps that begin with fact finding in order to identify or define a problem. Following this *diagnosis* step is that of considering alternative courses of action, followed by selecting a course of action, studying the consequences of the action, and identify what is learned (Susman & Evered, 1978). Integral to the model is the necessity of client/user participation, where small groups manage the action process (Cunningham 1976). This approach no longer calls for more applied research, nor for a form of research findings usable by practitioners. This new model does not deny the need for basic research, but has substantial implications for a new outlook on the teaching and practice of architecture where design research, design paticipation, and design development are inextricably linked activites (Figure 4.1). It is essentially necessary that behavioral research and programming

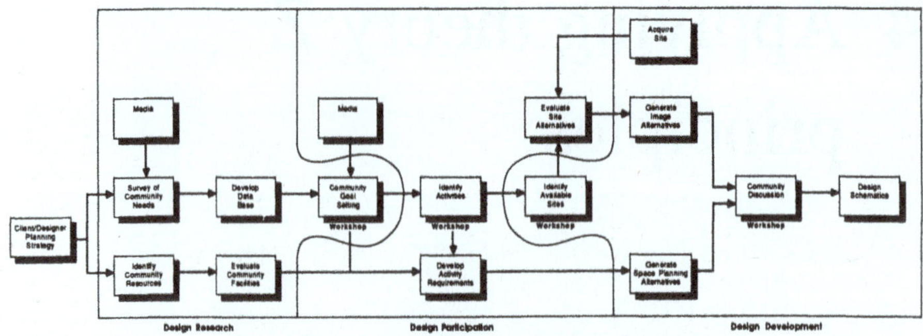

Figure 4.1 Participatory design process

become interdependent processes that are integrated with user participation.

The rationale for a new professional outlook is not necessarily unique to architecture, but to the ubiquitous gulf between academics and professionals, between theoreticians and practitioners, or between researchers and designers, in all fields. While there have been valiant efforts by many disciplines to 'bridge the gap,' there still remains a gulf between the fund of available knowledge and the application of this knowledge. In a similar way, conventional architectural practice usually undervalues the expertise of the user and denies their involvement in decision making. Traditionally, architects focus on the formal and visual issues and give less attention to the behavioral factors that may equally influence the form of the building. Albrecht (1988) concludes that the problems encountered by participatory design consist of different values and opposing taste cultures between architects and clients. He asserts that compromise may not be conducive to convincing design solutions, and that the architects role is often reduced to a facilitating activity, and attributes many of the shortcomings of effective participation to a lack of a theoretical framework. Thus, it is the intention of this section to develop an explanatory theory and examples of action research in an architectural arena.

The model proposed by the author is based on the belief that people who use the environment, who are the traditional subjects of research, become active participants in the research and equally active participants in changing the environment. This idea is predicated on the view that people who use the environment have an expertise equal to, but different than the expertise of the architect. Participation then becomes a central component of the research approach. Users would then be involved in evaluating research results and subsequently develop recommendations about how to address problems that have been identified.

Theory Z emphasizes participatory management in an wholistic atmosphere, where the culture of an organization is considered. In order to implement changes, it is necessary to understand the organization's culture. Type Z organizations function similar to an open system, where there is continual interaction with the environment, and a state of balance or harmony is achieved. Interaction with the environment implies listening, but may also necessitate internal adjustments within the organizations structure. Corporate CEO's are discovering that to implement changes they must first know the organization culture before introducing such techniques as quality circles, a form of teaming and participatory management. The quality circle is a participative management tool designed to systematically harness the brain power of employee's to solve an organization's problems of productivity and quality. Quality circles are different than committee's or task forces since leaders and members are trained in specific techniques of the circle process, including brainstorming and consensus decision making. The circle itself determines what problems will be analyzed and solved.

This theory and approach opens the way for people to find and pursue points of communality involving their own interests and those of the organizations for which they work. People do indeed gain satisfaction from feeling competent, in control, and free to choose for themselves. Personal involvment in the design of their workplace will aid the development of responsibility, cooperation, and self-motivation.

This action approach offers architects concerned with user needs a new set of social science tools. These new tools not only provide architects with a deeper understanding of the human condition, but an opportunity for engaging in an effective dialogue with people who use the environment. This approach is in contrast to the use of more casual methods of inquiry which typically reveal what is already obvious, or traditional social science approaches which tend to generalize people's requirements.

In a study reported in the Herman Miller magazine, ***Ideas,*** Sommer (1979) noted that allowing employees to select their own furniture from sample items of furniture assembled in a vacant warehouse resulted in a layout that was decentralized, modest, and personal, with the individual station at its core. The office had an unplanned quality to it as the total environment arrangement evolved from the sum of individual decisions. Different employees had different equipment and furnishings and were more satisfied with their work setting than were those in a comparable sample of employees who worked in a setting furnished from a single furniture system prescribed by expert space planners. Of particular interest here is that the warehouse building has been denied design awards while the later has received several. One juror described his denial of the award on the basis of the plan's 'residential quality' and 'lack of discipline and control of the interiors.' In the latter case, visual order and social control becomes the goal, not productivity or user satisfaction. The argument that employees want everyone treated in a visibly identical fashion does not hold up when employees participate in a procedure that allows them a genuine opportunity to make informed choices. Similarly, the appearance of order is based on the premise that the designed environment is created for users that are more or less identical. Yet, we have seen from the results of this and other research that there are many differences among individuals, and that these differences should be reflected in the complexity and variation of processes of environmental support applied to them.

Numerous examples of integrating Theory Z principles into design activity have been developed by the author. The following cases are presented in an abstracted version to illustrate how different techniques can be applied to a variety of design and planning situations.

Activity planning

An application of this process occurred during the planning for the Durham Arts Council (DAC) housed in a vacated City Hall building. After five years of occupancy the Council secured funds to make the spatial modifications that would suit the work flow of the organization. When the community needs had been identified and priorities established for the types of activities and events that were represented by the arts center, it was necessary to survey the adequacy of existing spaces in order to establish future space needs. Every organization included in the Arts Center facility was surveyed for their particular space requirements. This procedure was instituted by the Arts Council in order for participating organizations to have a stake in the process and the resulting decisions.

In a preliminary study of user's satisfaction with their present environment, often referred to as a post-occupancy evaluation (Wener, 1989), a survey was conducted with the DAC staff, members of affiliate organizations, and independent artists who rent studios, totalling 14 people. Understanding the organization and its purpose was the focus of the study. Although there was an attempt to assess the adequacy of their present space, the results showed that DAC places the highest emphasis on the provision of service to the community through art classes and cultural events. The members' perception of the organizational goals was identical to its chartered goals. Staff members were also asked to record their activities, the adequacy of the places where they were performed, the organization of the flow of information, and the nature of the social environment. The results of the study showed that many of the workplaces were described as being too small while the social environment was described as friendly and cooperative.

Environmental conditions related to light, temperature, and ventilation contributed to people's satisfaction with their job. Similarly, places that were too warm or poorly ventilated were reported to have a direct impact on job performance and satisfaction. Since the building occupants had identified many serious malfunctions in their work environment, a procedure was developed by the design team to permit the users to the redesign their work spaces. This was accomplished by organizing work groups and providing them with plans of their existing three-story building along with a sheet of graphic symbols corresponding to spatial activities.

Participants were then required to examine their workspace needs, estimate area requirements, and prepare a plan layout for each of the three floors of the existing building (Figure 4.2A). Each of the three participant groups proposed opposing solutions which they compared, and evaluated along with the design team, in order to arrive at a solution that would reconcile their differences. This approach permitted the building occupants to share their experiences and spatial concerns with each other through a process of collaborative planning. The results from all groups were summarized as shown on Figure 4.2B, and served as a point of further discussion. Finally, the design team prepared a layout (Figure 4.2C) that satisfied the space and adjacency requirements, as well as other related concerns voiced by the participants. The solution was accepted as a natural evolution of the architect/client collaborative effort, and not as the architect's ideas that needed to be accepted or rejected.

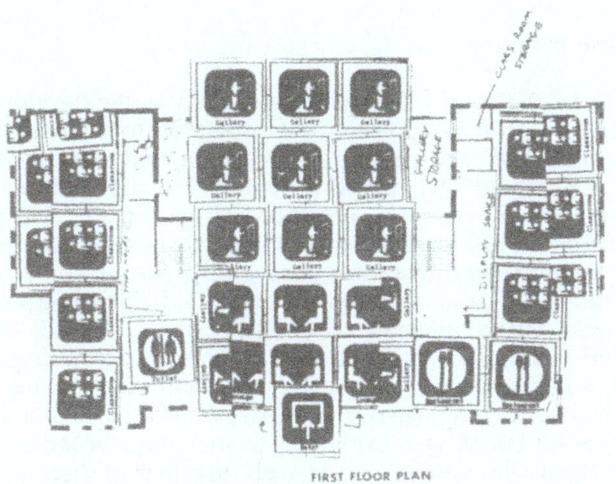

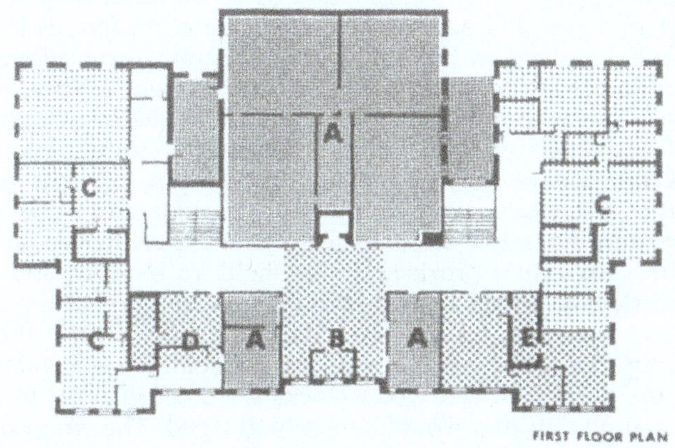

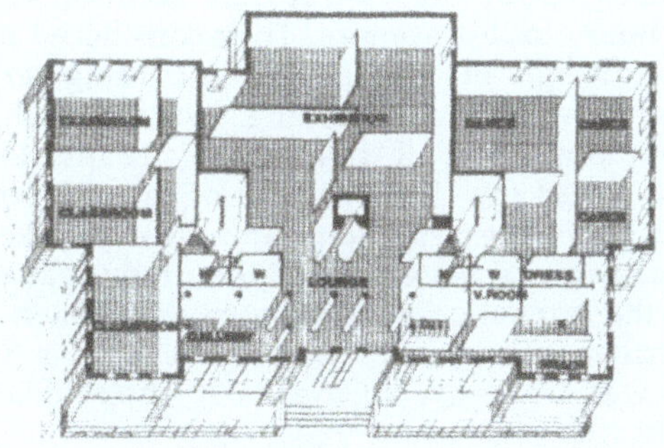

Figure 4.2 Transformation of first floor plan of arts center

Collaborative site planning

In another case, the choice of a collaborative strategy in the development of a children's center at SUNY Stony Brook was prompted by a division between university administration, and parents and teaching staff who were part of a corporation that operated their present facility. The rift between the two groups was largely due to poor communication during a sequence of unfulfilled administrative promises and unclear expectations between parties. Since the organizational structure and goals of a university are different from those of a campus child care center, a dialogue between groups could foster administrative understanding (Ellsworth & Leonard, 1988). In an effort to prevent the university-community gulf from expanding, a participatory process was proposed where the responsibility for making decisions rested with those with competence and expertise in a particular area. As a result, the corporate board was expanded to include a broad spectrum of parents and teachers who volunteered to work together to discuss, plan, and evaluate design options reflecting all facets of a child care center.

The present facility, which accommodated 65 children in three adjacent houses located in a wooded site, had been in operation for over ten years. Staff and parents involved in this innovative program were adamant about retaining the intimacy, scale, and quality of their present facility, in spite of the university administration's endorsement of a needs assessment that would increase its capacity to 200 children. Since the existing site could not adequately accommodate the expansion, the campus planner offered an alternate site that was strategically located near parking and a major campus circulation corridor. Since the site plan was the most controversial aspect of the new facility, an initial workshop was held to explore site planning options. This workshop was facilitated by the author (Figure 4.3).

Parents and teaching staff met at the children's center and worked together in groups of four with the aid of preassembled site planning kits developed by the author. Scaled wood blocks were constructed to provide a three dimensional quality that would be easily grasped. The wood blocks corresponded to all room areas and playrooms. Workgroups manipulated the pieces into various combinations of age group playroom arrangements until they reached consensus about the appropriate solution (Figure 4.4). The groups devoted two hours to this exercise. They considered many issues that would influence the design of the facility, including solar orientation, circulation, age group clustering, and parking. Not surprisingly, each group arrived at similar solutions. They all divided the site into locations for four separate buildings, to reflect the characteristics of their present facility. They admitted reservations about their solutions, and also remarked that the scale and complexity of the exercise were greater than they realized. Each group struggled to achieve the separation and autonomy contained in their present arrangement. All participants agreed that they reached a point where the architect's expertise was necessary to evaluate their ideas, and to solve problems beyond their capacity.

Follow-up work sessions consisted of playroom organization concepts for different age groups and subsequent alternative building design solutions proposed by the author. Three schemes were developed for group discussion, all of which were based on the ideas generated at the first site planning workshop (Figure 4.5). Rather than the four isolated single focus buildings, that appeared in the parent-teachers original solution, there was unanimous support for a proposal consisting of a single building with separate entrances to achieve the desired autonomy contained in their present facility.

From the university administration's viewpoint, the collaborative strategy improved relations between all groups, and provided a new channel of communication for parents and staff to share their child related expertise. All voices were heard during the sessions, and while there was not always total agreement with decisions, there was general acceptance that the process was fair and open. Involving user groups in the space planning process sensitizes the participants to the complexities and conflicts that architects are required to resolve. By experiencing the trade-offs necessary for making proximity decisions, participants realized how critical time was for achieving satisfactory solutions. The direct experience of making space planning decisions in small groups permitted many ideas to be considered. While the schematic floor plans generated by each group were different, they did reflect a serious effort at identifying important activities and their relationships. Clearly, the trust established between the participants and the architect created a healthier climate, an ingredient characteristic in a Theory Z approach.

Figure 4.3 Site plans generated by work groups

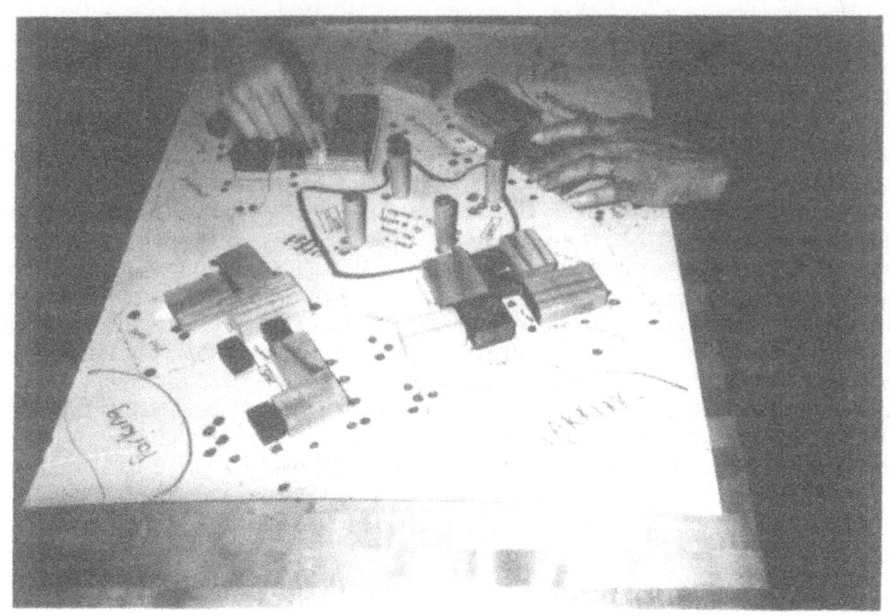

Figure 4.4 Wood blocks used to develop the site plan

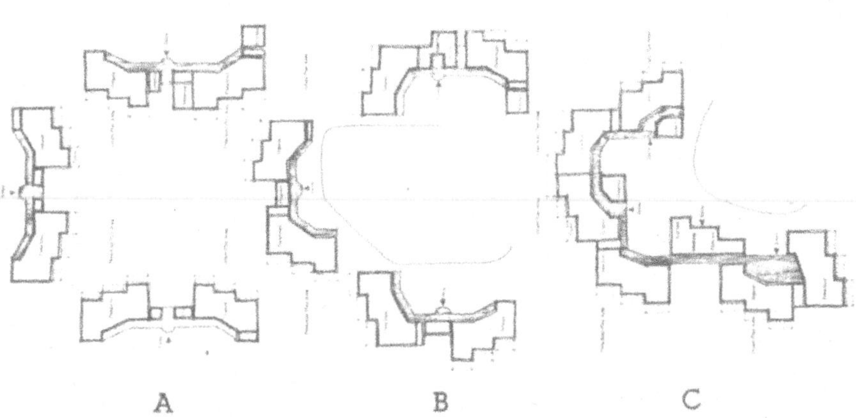

Figure 4.5 Alternative site plans prepared by the architect

School self assessment

In a more general way, a self assessment process was developed for citizen groups, teachers, and policy makers to interview, observe, and discuss ways and means of making middle schools more responsive to the developmental needs of young adolescents. This self assessment process was develped in conjunction with the Center for Early Adolescence (Dorman, 1981), a national advocate and resource center for parents and policy makers. The goal was to develop an action oriented process for school improvement. An assessment process was developed to take a comprehensive look at middle-grade schools to see how the academic and developmental needs of young adolescents are accommodated by the physical facilities, the school climate, and the teaching program. The assessment program consisted of a series of interview schedules for use with the principal, teachers, counselors, students, and parents. In addition to interviews, an observation form was developed to gain a more comprehensive understanding of the school environment. Observations were required of the physical facilities where such items as places for socialization, spatial flexibility, and opportunities for students to personalize their school, were noted (Figure 4.6). Observations of the classroom centered around the ability for students to direct their own studies, and modify the classroom to suit their own needs.

To stimulate more participation among school community members, design aids were developed to increase their awareness to the architectural implications of the school environment. Unless a teacher understands why one room arrangement may be superior to another, all the physical changes in the world will have little or no impact on the nature of the learning process within the classroom. The design aids included photographs of a variety of school settings that were associated with appropriate activities generated from educational goals deemed relevant by the teachers. Mixed groups of teachers, parents, and policy makers discussed and agreed on commonly accepted objectives, and activities that were matched to the photographs. Similarly, photographs of different school settings were rated by community members for the positive or negative features they evoked.

The self assessment process is usually conducted by a team of six to eighteen school staff, parents, and a variety of other professionals, usually selected by the principal. In some instances students participated in the assessment by interviewing the students. Many schools across the country have participated in school improvement projects. The schools all vary in size, physical facilities, location, and socioeconomic make-up of the student body, yet these factors have not been deterrents if educators want to improve their schools. Many schools have reported that while in the process of doing their assessments, spontaneous changes were occurring. For example, there was more positive interaction between teachers and students; more interest in the school among students, parents, and staff; and more specific behavioral objectives from teachers. The assessment gives teachers a sanctioned method to participate in setting priorities for the school. The result is staff members who feel empowered to make their school a better place and who are committed to reaching agreed upon goals. The school assessment process is similar to a Type Z organization, where the expertise of all people involved in the school setting contribute to the social, administrative, and physical changes.

Observation Form

Need	PHYSICAL FACILITIES	Yes	No
C	1. Building is neat, clean, and in good repair. There are few, if any, signs of vandalism or graffiti.		
P	2. Student work is displayed on bulletin boards, walls, tables in classes and other areas throughout the building.		
SE	3. Pictures and displays depict various racial and ethnic groups.		
SE	4. Pictures, posters, and displays show both boys and girls engaged in a wide variety of activities, for example: girls as doctors, policewomen, construction workers; boys as nurses, social workers, secretaries; girls playing baseball and boys cooking.		
P	5. Announcements are posted by students and staff about activities and concerns.		
D	6. The building itself is flexible, including some large open spaces, some small rooms. Some spaces are multifunctional.		
D	7. Furniture throughout the school is movable.		
SE	8. There are quiet places for individuals, pairs, and groups of students to withdraw, relax, and think, such as student lounges or reading lofts.		
Phy	9. There are identified places where students can be noisy and engage in physical activity.		
Phy	10. There is plenty of room in corridors and classrooms for movement from one place to another.		
D	11. There is outdoor space for projects such as science gardens and building projects. It is being used.		
P	12. Students contribute to the upkeep and appearance of the school. For example, they may build furniture, clean their own tables in the cafeteria, pick up trash, decorate bulletin boards.		
SE	13. There are doors or curtains on the stalls in the bathrooms and dressing rooms.		

COMMENTS:

Figure 4.6 Physical facilities observation form

Child development center: A case study

This section describes the way in which research findings can be integrated into the design process. The techniques described are based on the results of personal experiences in designing and programming child care facilities. Earlier experience suggests the need for a new approach that can engage the architect and the client/ user group in a process that links children's developmental needs to facility requirements. Strategies are described that engage parents, teachers, and administrators in collaboration with the architect during the initial stages of design. This process has produced teachers with new capabilities in playroom planning and organization, as well as with an understanding of the way in which architects make decisions. Although the example described is a campus child care facility, the techniques can be generalized for other types of facilities as well. Integral to the process, is the concept of the non-paying client. For programming purposes, people who use the building are the clients of the architect, whether or not they pay for services. Reference to the user as the non-paying client then, attaches greater significance to the importance of user contributions, and to a more binding relationship between the paying and non-paying client.

Programming and design consultation were requested by the planning group of a proposed 75 child facility and training center for Wake Community College's, Child Development Program, in North Carolina. They contacted the Community Development Group, North Carolina State University, for design assistance. Since this facility was intended as a demonstration site for the county, the department head and client representative, the teaching staff, and the educational consultants to the program, were anxious to follow a planning process in which research findings, their expertise, and educational philosophy, would be linked to design decisions.

The diagram in Figure 4.1 describes the integration of three major components of the collaborative design process; *design research, design participation, and design development*. These components precede production, construction, and evaluation. In this model, programming represents the synthesis between design research and design participation. This collaborative design process is a departure from traditional programming appproaches since the client, the non-paying client, and the architect are directly involved in all decision making stages. Furthermore, the stages described as design research and design participation subsume what is normally referred to as facility programming. This distinction enables the identification of discreet activities for each stage, as well as clarifying the difference between information received from secondary sources, such as surveys and data bases, and from primary sources such as direct, face-to-face involvement.

Typically, institutional client groups planning the child care center initiate a formal needs assessment that includes the following steps:

1. Campus survey of student child care needs.
2. Survey of campus child care centers.
3. Site visits to child care facilities.
4. Consultation with child care experts.
5. Departmental Planning.

The above steps constitute the *design research* phase of the collaborative design process. The *design research* phase included a needs assessment, visits to other child care centers, and the establishment of educational goals which included desired staff child ratios and other factors inherent in a high quality center. Although typically initiated by the client, the architect can often provide guidelines for more systematic fact finding procedures. Surveys and visits to existing facilities, if properly organized, can reveal valuable insights into their functions, since casual visits often reveal obvious results.

Research findings

Since needs assessment studies often yield conclusions far in excess of what is practical or feasible, the most important planning decision for the child care center is the number of children to be served. Research studies (Kritchevsky, Prescott, & Walling, 1974) have shown that the developmental quality of child care services drops sharply with increases in the number of children served in one building. Prescott, Jones, Kritchevsky, Milich, & Haselhoef (1975) found that center size was a reliable predictor of program quality. In centers which served over 60 children, major emphasis tended to be placed on rules and routine guidance. Prescott et al. (1975) also found that large centers rarely offered children the experience of participating in wide age-range groups. Mixing of ages in smaller centers offered opportunities for older children to serve as models and to enrich overall play possibilities (Moore, Lane, Hill, Cohen, and McGinty, 1989).

The age groups generally served by most centers are infants (six weeks to 12 months), toddlers (12 months to two years), and preschoolers (three to five years). In order to achieve the needed critical number in each age group, a target number of 60 to 75 children is recommended (Moore, Lane, Hill, Cohen, and McGinty, 1989) as a basic planning module. As the institutional needs increase, the number of children should then be increased in multiples of 60 to 75 administratively independent units, to keep the scale of the facility within the child's grasp.

In addition to the number of children in a center, an adequate amount of space for children's activities is necessary to ensure a quality developmentally oriented program. In a commission study for the federal government, based on a review of cases of density and behavior in child-care settings, Prescott and David (1976) recommended a minimum of 42 square feet of usable floor space per child. Cohen, Moore, and McGinty (1978), in conducting interviews as part of their national research, suggested that 42 square feet per child permits a much more flexible program, allowing simultaneous options in active and quiet pursuits without children disturbing each other. A study by Rohe and Nuffer (1977) showed that while increasing spatial density by reducing space tended to increase aggressive behavior, sheltering activity areas by inserting partitions increased cooperative behavior. Both density and partitioning affected children's activity choices (Rohe & Nuffer, 1977). In a review of studies, Moore et al. (1989) concluded that the most desirable social environment occurs at a density of 42 to 50 square feet of usable activity space per child. These research findings provide the basis for facility size and playroom organization criteria.

Design participation

During this stage of the process, background research findings are integrated into the activity analysis. Accompanying the area requirement for usable activity space for each child, is the need for well defined areas limited to one learning activity, with clear boundaries from circulation space and from other activity areas (Moore, 1986). Well-defined activity areas or centers may be created with surrounding partitions, storage cabinets, changes in floor levels and surface materials, or other visual elements that suggest boundaries. Spatially well defined areas support social interaction, cooperative behavior, and exploratory behavior (Moore, 1986; Smith & Connolly, 1980). Well-defined areas also prevent ongoing play from being disrupted by intruders (Field, 1980). Running and chasing activities are common in classrooms where boundaries are not well defined. Conversely, well defined activity centers, with clear boundaries from circulation space and from other activity areas, and with some visual or acoustic separation, decrease classroom interruptions, and contribute to longer attention spans (Moore et al., 1989). This implies that activity centers within the classroom require a high degree of spatial definition. The design task, requires the development of a building program that can spatially respond to the developmental goals of the teachers of young children, as well as to the literature on child development.

Modeling the playroom

Since the playroom is the basic spatial unit of a children's center, prior familiarity with its organization can enable teachers to enter into a productive dialogue with the architect. Modeling the playroom is an activity developed for a teachers workshop that allows participants to manipulate fixed and movable playroom elements in order to achieve the desired developmental objectives. Working in teams of three people each, teachers are assigned a design task to create a playroom for a specific age group, such as infants, or toddlers. Found materials, including cardboard, wood blocks, styrofoam, construction paper, and plastic are provided along with instructions to the teachers for measuring and cutting the materials needed to construct a three-dimensional model. The model making is preceded by an exercise where developmental objectives and corresponding activity areas for specific age groups are discussed and agreed upon by each team. Model results are discussed by participants, then playrooms are joined together to resemble a building for different age groups. At this juncture, issues of playroom adjacencies, building flow, and location of services are discussed by participants (Figure 4.7) in an exercise of four hours in duration. Playroom modeling is an effective method for preparing the client group to actively and constructively participate in planning a child development center.

Recording activity data

Planning began with focusing on the child as the basic unit of development. Next, the design participation phase involved the collection of behavioral data relating to each activity in which infants, toddlers, and preschoolers would be engaged. The conceptual framework used for the design of the facility was the activity center (Sanoff & Sanoff, 1988). The teaching staff of the child development training program identified the developmental objectives for each activity by age group, and the 'molecular' activities that would occur in the activity center (Figure 4.8).

The water play area, for example, the objectives of which would include sensory and perceptual acuity, concept formation, and eye hand coordination (Sanoff & Sanoff, 1988; Weinstein, 1987), would include such molecular activities as pouring, measuring, mixing, and floating objects, all of which are related to the primary activity. Activity data sheets were prepared to record the relevant activity information which served as a program, and resource for future decisions. The data sheets provided a format where specific equipment needs could also be identified for future purchasing.

Spatial planning

Since the planning of a child care facility also reflects a particular ideology about child development, a space planning exercise was developed to engage the teaching staff in decisions related to playroom layout. Since a planning guide of 50 square feet of usuable space per child limited the number of activity centers that could be included in a playroom, scenarios were written by teachers about a typical child's day. The constraints encouraged the teaching staff to use 'trade-offs' effectively since they were required to decide which activity centers were most important for various age groups. Graphic symbols corresponding to each activity center (Figure 4.9) enabled the manipulation of children's movement patterns in the playroom. This was the first step in providing environmental information to foster mental image development (Hunt, 1985). Spatially organizing activity centers on a'game board' corresponding to a playroom, permitted the determination of which centers were to be fixed and which flexible. The spatial layout process required teachers to consider planning concepts, adjacency requirements, circulation, and visual and acoustic privacy between activity centers. Most of all, the process reinforced the concept of activity centers.

The teachers worked through a playroom layout by manipulating activity symbols for each age group. They outlined the flow process from entering the facility, greeting the staff, disrobing in the cubbie area, and moving to various activity centers. When planning the infant room, the teachers identified the diaper change as the focal point with surveillance to all other activity areas. To avoid the clustering of unsightly cribs, the teachers proposed decentralizing the sleeping activity into several crib alcoves. This process entailed small group discussions that required consensus in all decisions. When agreement was reached, the symbols were fastened to the base to constitute a record of the group's decisions. Cardboard scale models of each playroom, with movable walls and furniture, were then constructed by the designer, corresponding with the flow patterns in the diagrams developed by the teachers (Figure 4.10). This stage of the process permitted the teaching staff to visualize the three dimensional implications of their decisions. Schematic models of the playrooms limited the amount of information

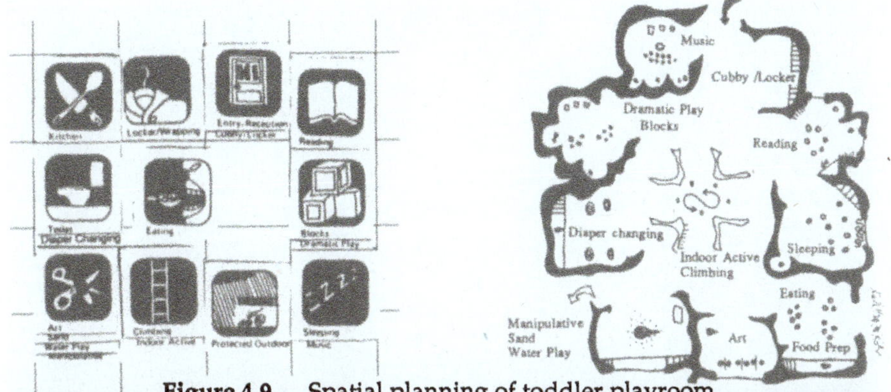

Figure 4.9 Spatial planning of toddler playroom

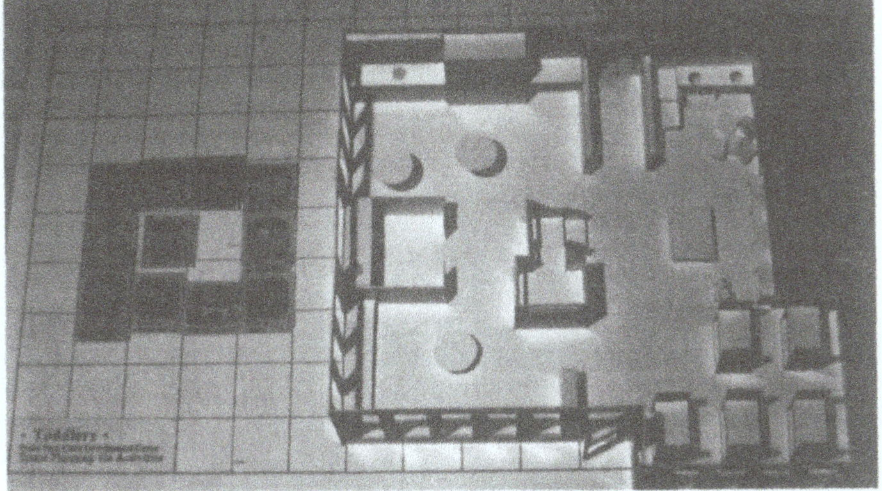

Figure 4.10 Model of toddler playroom

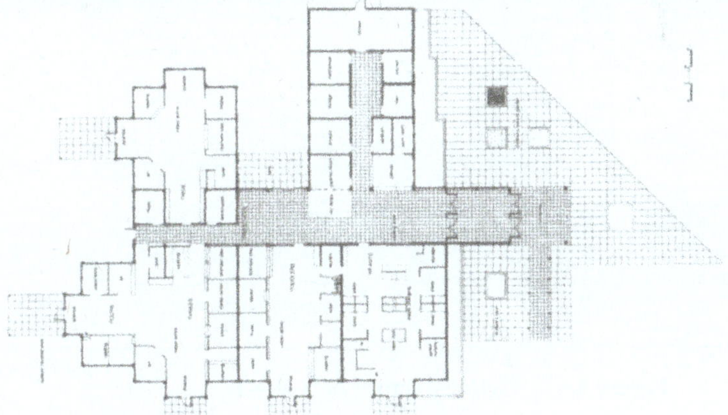

Figure 4.11 Plan of children's center

Figure 4.7 Classroom planning teacher's workshop

Toddler

In this activity center the toddlers can learn about the properties of sand and water. The reaction of both to human manipulation and their flexible properties make them excellent tools for learning about natural forces. Manipulative toys need semi-private play environments so that the child can focus on the skill without major distraction. This hands-on type format for learning requires space that promotes this concept.

Manipulative
Sand
Water Play

100 square feet

Objectives

Sensory-motor; fine motor skills
Cognitive,math,visual motor
Socialization
Concept formation:math,science, cognition,self-help, language
Social skills
Building fine and gross motor
Relaxation

Notes

Outer rim on table for support and placement of toys
Child safe hooks for hanging toys
Water safe floor
Floor seating

Equipment	Storage Open	Storage Closed
12 transparent bins for objects	•	
Horizontal floor level work surface	•	
Wall display surface-interlocking toys	•	
Vertical display		
Storage for 24 extra bins		•
Pegboard storage..Puzzles		•
Floor height sand table with rim	•	
Storage for toys		•
Alternative materials storage		
Floor-level water table w/cover	•	
Storage for towels and toys		•
Smock hanging space	•	
Mop closet		•
Horizontal display for concept pictures	•	

Acoustical level- Moderate
Moderately private

Figure 4.8 Activity center data sheet

presented at one time, conveying only the most significant issues in order to minimize information overload(Hunt,1985).Teachers could reconsider earlier decisions, particularly when they saw conflicts arise that were not easily predicted in the two-dimensional diagrams. Although circulation between activity centers was considered in the development of the activity symbol diagrams, the scale model conveyed the need to establish clear boundaries between centers to prevent distraction, while permitting the teacher an unobstructed view of all children's play areas. The scale models included information not shown on the activity diagrams, such as furniture and equipment, but the movable pieces were easily manipulated by the teachers as they referred to the activity data sheets.

When the teachers reached agreement about the best playroom arrangement, form diagrams were developed by the designer, elaborating on their spatial decisions (Figure 4.11). These diagrams combined activity centers into playrooms for different age groups. The diagrams allowed teachers to gain an understanding of 'conceptual relationships.' Teachers were better able visualize how educational objectives could be enhanced through the design of playrooms.

Design criteria

The results of the participatory exercises helped to generate design criteria, as well as to modify the requirements of the building program. Several statements were developed to describe the fundamental environmental characteristics of an effective child development center. They are as follows:

> *The environment must be comfortable and inviting for children and adults. It should reflect an atmosphere conducive to children's growth. Materials and equipment should be easily accessible to children in order to encourage independence and self esteem. An effective means of organizing the environment is to develop interest centers where the playroom is divided into areas that focus on specific activities. It is advisable that quieter activity areas be placed in close proximity in order to promote a quiet atmosphere. Activity areas demand visual clarity and well defined limits if children are expected to interpret cues on appropriate areas for certain types of play. A quality playroom would include the following activity areas:*

- creative expression/art
- literature/language art
- dramatic play/housekeeping
- block building
- self-image, personal hygiene
- science and exploration
- cooking
- water play
- carpentry
- manipulative
- music and movement

More specific guidelines that influenced the final solution included:

- •protected outdoor play area adjacent to each playroom
- •south orientation for playroom and adjacent outdoor area
- •daylight to be provided by rooftop glazing and glazing orientation.

Facility design

The teaching staff was involved in organizing the building components into a facility design, using graphic symbols that corresponded to the major areas, such as playrooms, kitchen, offices, corridors, and lobby area. Age group adjacencies were considered, with opportunities for different age groups to have visual contact with each other. This was achieved in many ways, including low windows in each playroom for children to be able to see into the adjacent room. The planning concept that emerged from the discussions was that of a 'central spine' from which playrooms would be connected. The spine would be more than a corrider, yet similar to a street, where parents, teachers, and visitors could view into the playrooms observing children's activities (Figure 4.12). To emphasize the street concept, it was necessary to fill the area with daylight through the use of overhead skylights. Each of the playrooms, too, would have a central spine leading to a covered outdoor play area. Spatially well defined activity centers were located on either side of the playroom spine. These playrooms included fixed areas for art and water play, and centers that could change their focus at the descretion of the teacher. Spatially well defined centers implies the need to be distinctly different from adjacent centers. This differentiation was characterized by physical features such as partially surrounding dividers or storage units, implied boundaries through the use of columns, changes in floor level or ceiling height, changes in floor covering, and changes in light levels. Learning materials, furniture and equipment also contribute to the distinctiveness of the activity centers.

Teachers response to the process

The diagrams and scale models provided a clear sequential procedure where all decisions could be traced and subsequently modified. The teachers, however, found difficulty in comprehending the consequences of many spatial decisions. While they were able to follow the process of playroom organization, they had difficulty visualizing the implications of alternative playroom arrangements. A continual reference to scale models and perspective drawings aided the teachers substantially in contributing their expertise to the design of the building. The teachers remarked that this process provided them with a better understanding of the principles of spatial planning, and the role of the architect. They experienced the 'ripple effect,' where minor changes in adjacency relationships manifest themselves into major revisions in the spatial layout of the playroom, or of the building. This diagnostic procedure of examining flow processes and linking objectives to activity centers, enables teachers to develop a conceptual understanding of playroom and building layout principles.

Figure 4.12 Interior views of children's center

Conclusion

The interaction between teachers and the designer described in this project is clearly a departure from the traditional approach to facility development. Conventional practice usually denies the expertise of the user (non-paying client) and their involvement in design decision making. Traditional designers also focus on the formal and visual issues and give less attention to the behavioral factors that may equally influence the form of the building. Facility designers typically consider defining relationships between playrooms and other areas, disadvantaging the teaching staff because of their inability to comprehend floor plans and the consequences of spatial decisions. The teachers' expertise occurs at the level of the children's behavioral interactions within the playroom, but this factor is usually considered after occupancy of the facility.

A structured process was provided to enable child development professionals to lend their expertise to the initial programming stages of the design process. Use of activity data sheets, activity symbols, and form diagrams permitted the designer to integrate knowledge about children's behavior and their requirements into a format that was conducive to making space planning decisions. Integrating the expertise of the staff in this structured process established clear linkages between child development goals, and the types of places where these goals could be fulfilled. The teaching staff's continual involvement in the building design process encouraged the exchange of ideas and concepts with the designer, which increased the staff's ability to act as effective design team members. The active part of the process usually terminates with the schematic design of the children's center, which is the result of the team's involvement.

The effectiveness of a collaborative process is contingent upon the involvement of the architect from the inception of the project. When the architect is an integral part of the process, the building design proposals are clearly understood by the user/client group of teaching staff, parents, and administrators. On those occasions when the program is completed prior to the architect being commissioned for the project, significant communication problems can occur between the user group and the architect. In this instance, the architect of record, Haskins, Rice, Savage & Pearce, PA, was appointed by the college administration after the program and preliminary design had been completed by the consulting design team. Although considerable effort was made by the design team and teaching staff to explain the rationale for the design decisions, the architect could not easily comprehend the nuances of the proposed design solution. Similarly, the architects drawings were not understood by the teaching staff, since they were prepared for construction purposes. This created difficulty in the working relations with the client because the architect often urged quick approval to expedite the process.

The language of the program should reflect the concepts developed by the teaching staff and conveyed in terms of educational goals and children's activities. The language of the architect-the floor plans and elevations-are the interpretation of verbal concepts, and are often untelligible to the user group, especially if they are not developed simultaneously with the program. The implications of these experiences are that ownership in the design process, achieved through active involvement in design decisions, permits the user/ non-paying client to exercise free and informed choice. The separation of the programming and design stages not only limits participation of a wide range of experts, but jeopardizes the ability of the product to fulfill the expectations of the program.

Acknowledgment

The success of this project is due to Joan Sanoff, Department Head, Early Childhood Development, Wake Technical Community College, who participated in the programming and design development phases. Thanks, also to James Utley, for his design work. An earlier version of this work appeared in *Children's Environments Quarterly*, (Winter, 1989) 6, 4: 32-39. Another version is in Preiser, W.F.E. (ed.), 1993, *Professional Practice in Facility Programming*, Van Nostrand Reinhold, New York.

Planning outdoor play

Planning for outdoor play is an integral part of the design process and is a vital component of the child care center. Typically perceived as a staging area for large muscle development, the outdoor play area is not only important for the child's health but contributes to the child's learning experiences (Threlfall, 1986). Outdoor play space offers opportunities for adventure, challenge, and wonder in the natural environment (Frost & Klein, 1983). The only substantial difference between indoor and outdoor activity is that one has a roof over it. Both, however, need architectural and landscape definition, and both need to provide for the multiplicity of children's developmental needs. For example, a play yard with 12 tricycles, a rocking boat, a tumble tub, a jungle gym, a dirt area, and a sand table with water, has 17 separate play units but only four different kinds of things to do (Kritchevsky, Prescott, & Walling, 1974). Variety can be an important measure of interest. Also, complexity, or the number of subparts of a piece of equipment, such as a sandbox with play materials, water, climbing boards, and crates, can add to a child's interest.

The process of creating outdoor play spaces is age group oriented and began with developmental objectives that help to generate the activities in which children engage (Sanoff & Sanoff 1982). The teaching staff and design team work together to establish linkages between objectives for outdoor play, the related children's activities, and the play settings required (Figure 4.13) .

To complement the indoor environment, the outdoors provides play settings that stress muscle development as well as natural settings to provide experience in the life cycle of plants and animals. The props used to enable the teachers to make spatial decisions included drawings of different play settings as well as statements of objectives and lists of activities. The planning group moves through a series of collaborative stages in which all members try to reach consensus. Finally, the activities and play settings are organized into play zones which range from passive to active play, and from private to group activities. This part of the planning process helps to generate discussions about the purpose of outdoor play, usually dispelling many of the myths surrounding large muscle development as the primary purpose of children's outdoor activities (Figure 4.14).

Learning objectives for outdoor play are discussed in a similar way to those in the planning of the playrooms. Objectives such as problem solving, concept development, and social development, are key concerns of the teachers. Supporting activities like role playing, climbing, feeling and handling, balancing, sliding, and construction comprise the array of choices most frequently made. As a result of making these linkages, the subsequent choice of play equipment and play areas are based on a clear understanding of the developmental needs that the outdoor play area should serve. Other types of individual or quiet activities, group games, and opportunities for exercising imagination are also identified for outdoor use, but do not necessarily require the construction of special equipment.

An analysis of the building site and its topography will influence the location and options for various play settings which could be clustered according to similarity of requirements. Play zones include areas for drama nature, adventure, and large muscle development.

planning outdoor play

pop

Planning Outdoor play (POP) is a method of facilitating the design of children's outdoor play and the selection of appropriate equipment.

POP consists of four (4) sets of card categories:

OBJECTIVES (yellow cards)- the purpose of outdoor play
ACTIVITIES (orange cards)- what children do outdoors
ZONES (pink cards)- areas of related activities
SETTINGS (see POP sheets 4 & 5) equipment used by children

NOTE: YOU WILL NEED TO SUPPLY YOUR OWN CARDS, USING THE LISTED CATEGORIES ON POP sheet 7.

ACTIVITIES

mixing	painting
feeling & handling	cooking
hitting	pouring
crawling	stretching
splashing	sliding
role playing	constructing
dressing up	planting
molding	swinging
contact with animals	balancing
digging	vehicular motion
climbing	throwing & catching

OBJECTIVES

concept formation	social development
cooperation	initiative
problem solving	communication
emotional development	self expression
self confidence	positive self image
language development	perceptual development
sensory discrimination	sensory development
self motivation	

The game is to be played by one to four people (teachers, assistants, parents, etc.). To begin, each player selects four of the most important OBJECTIVE cards. After each player has chosen cards, the individual OBJECTIVE cards are pooled. Through negotiation, the group must choose from these, no more than four OBJECTIVE cards. Players are urged to forcefully support their individual choices, especially if other members did not make the same choice, until they persuade or are persuaded by others that an OBJECTIVE should be included in the final set. Use the game record sheet to report the final decision.

Next, as a group, examine each OBJECTIVE and select no more than three ACTIVITY cards that best satisfy each OBJECTIVE. Record all the selections.

Now, as a group, rearrange all the ACTIVITY cards (twelve) so they appear to fit into an appropriate ZONE. It is important to note that not all of the ZONE cards need to be used. Record all selections.

Finally, select the appropriate SETTING that corresponds with each of the ACTIVITY choices and record the number of the SETTING. The set of rules is only a guide for gaining insight into the planning process. Players should feel free to change the rules in order to accommodate more specific needs.

RECORD SHEET

OBJECTIVES

a ______
b ______
c ______
d ______

ACTIVITIES

a	b
1 ______	1 ______
2 ______	2 ______
3 ______	3 ______

c	d
1 ______	1 ______
2 ______	2 ______
3 ______	3 ______

Figure 4.13 Planning outdoor play process: Setting objectives

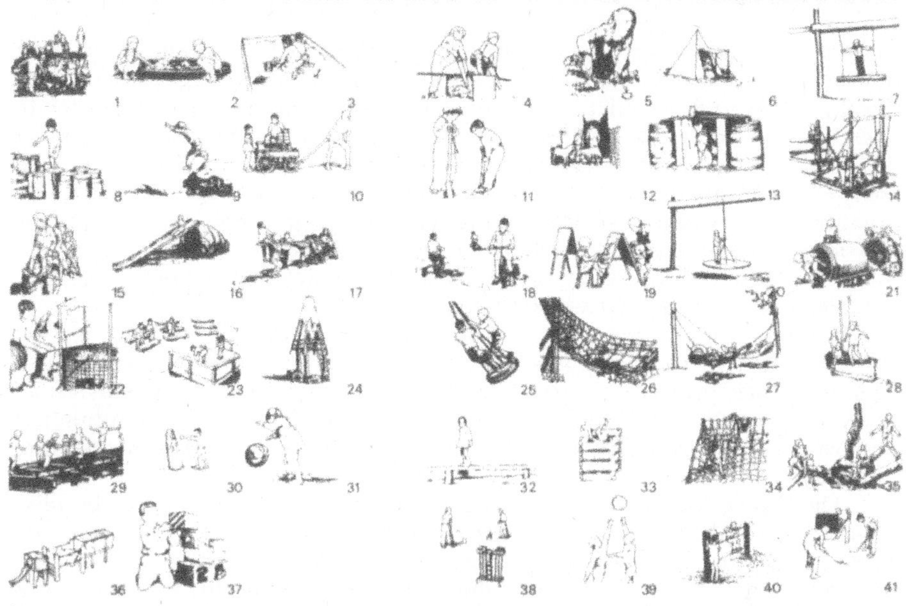

Equipment Options

ZONES	ACTIVITIES	SETTINGS
Creative Play Zone		
Imaginative Play Zone		
Dramatic Play Zone		
Nature Zone		
Adventure Play Zone		
Private Play Zone		
Manipulative Coordination Zone		
Large Muscle Development Zone		
Open Area Play Zone		

To save time, the cards should be prepared prior to the meeting at which you plan to play the game.

To make the cards, we suggest you use:

3 sheets of construction paper, 1 yellow, 1 orange, 1 pink
scissors and a felt tip pen

Cut the paper into one inch strips; cut the strips in half. Use the strips as playing cards. You will need 22 orange, 15 yellow, and 9 pink cards.

Figure 4.14 Planning outdoor play process: Equipment planning

Organizational self assessment: A case study

The Winston Salem Urban League project proposed to relocate an exisitng organization into new facilities. An information gathering process was developed to understand the operation of a small organization in order to design a suitable work environment. Through a systematic examination of different facets of the organization, the present office environment was analyzed in terms of: (1) the staff activities, and how they are related to the organization, its goals, structure, and system for producing work; (2) the reactions, perceptions, and attitudes of the staff towards their exisitng workplace. From this information it was possible to develop a plan to accommodate, and facilitate their work procedures.

The objective of this project was to develop a new office layout for the Winston Salem Urban League based on analysis of their existing facilities, as well as of their projected needs. The project involved an activity analysis, an analysis of the flow of office information, a network of staff communiation patterns, and a profile of each individual's activities and his/her spatial requirements.

The league had offices on the fourth floor of a downtown office building which the staff felt hindered their image and effectiveness in the community. They acquired a block of four buildings close to their present location, which provided direct street access, and the ability to combine their services with other community organizations. Of the 160,000 square feet available, the Urban League required 5400 square feet.

The Winston Salem Urban League is a non-profit community organization that is a local affiliate of the Urban League with headquarters in New York City. Their mission is to enable Afro-Americans and other minority group members to cultivate and exercise their full human potential by conducting programs in education, emloyment, housing, economic development, community development, and social welfare. The league conducts surveys and training programs, and furnishes technical assistance. The League has a policy making Board of Directors composed of people from the community. A professional staff carries on the day-to-day activities of the Urban League Movement. All of the professional staff were involved in the programming process which provided data, as well as interpreting their results.

Process

The effectiveness of an organization can be measured by the degree to which it accomplishes its goals. One argument for the careful delineation of goals is their use as criteria for evaluating the relative success or failure of the organization. Bennis (1966) the noted organization theorist, has proposed several criteria for evaluating an organization's effectiveness. In addition to problem solving ability, the extent to which the members of an organization know what they are trying to do and share perceptions concerning the nature of the organization, contribute to successful performance.

The need to formulate goals seems implicit in developing that sense of identity, which Bennis suggests is sharpest when four entities are congruent:

- The manifest organization (formally described in charts, rules, and policies).
- The assumed organization (the one the members would describe).
- The extant organization (the true system which could be revealed through systematic study).
- The requisite organization (based on and determined by the organization's purpose and goals).

Before any purposeful activity can occur towards solving spatial problems, an awareness of what this organization is trying to do is necessary, particularly if the design solution intends to facilitate the organization's purpose.

To this end, a questionnaire was developed and distributed to each of the staff members asking for the purpose of the organization as well as their individual work patterns (Figure 4.15). The findings from the questionnaire indicated that the major objectives of the organization stated by staff members were consistent with their charter and included such statements as the following:

- to provide education to the economically disadvantaged
- to provide employment opportunities
- to provide counselling to minorities on self confidence
- to encourage self sufficiency through employment
- to provide specialized services to the handicapped, displaced homemakers, and to youth
- to encourage non-traditional employment for women.

WINSTON-SALEM URBAN LEAGUE - OFFICE QUESTIONNAIRE
STEVEN CLIFF, METE GUREL
SEPTEMBER 28, 1981

Please describe the purpose of your organization.

Please briefly describe the nature of your work.

To what degree do you work individually? (Please circle one)

not at all — little — half of the time — often — always

How much of this work is, (Percentage)

reading?
writing reports?
telephoning?
other (please specify)
TOTAL

When working individually do you require acoustic privacy? (Please circle one)

often — sometimes — never

When working individually do you require visual privacy? (Please circle one)

often — sometimes — never

Who are the people you work most closely with? 1- 2-

Name the people you would enjoy working with the most.

1-
2-

How do you most frequently communicate? Personal contact / Memo / Inter-office memo / Telephone

If by personal contact, do you meet, In your work place? / In their office? / Other

Do you have any one on one contact with the people outside your organization?

often — sometimes — never

Do you have contacts with outside people as a group in the Urban League offices?

often — sometimes — never

How long do the meetings last?

less than 10 min. — 1/2 hr. — more than an hour

Do you need any special equipment for meetings? Yes___ No___

If yes then what do you require?

With whom do you have informal conversation in your work place?

1-
2-

Where else does informal conversation take place?

1-
2-

List the three things you like best about your work place.

1-
2-
3-

List the three things you like worst about your work place.

1-
2-
3-

NAME: DEPARTMENT: SUPERVISOR:

Figure 4.15 Office evaluation questionnaire

What actually occurred in the Urban League's current office was seen as a prerequisite for designing the type of environment to contain the system. In this sense, information pertaining to behavior in the organization such as types of activities, particular locations and places, and particular persons was collected. This information was necessary to describe the 'behavioral network' in order to develop workplace requirements.

Specific data was required in order to avoid the traditional shortcomings of asking a department head or manager to prepare listings of staff needs. A detailed account of work processes, storage and display needs, generated a large quantity of information that was best handled by the use of standardized forms (Figure 4.16).

The individual workplace was the basic unit of analysis for the study of personal requirements, though in large organizations personal requirements would not substantially change the nature of the workplace. This situation is particularly evident in organizations with large changes in personnel.

In addition to the workplace requirements, information was obtained on the space needs for group meetings, special equipment, and storage. An examination of the Urban League's existing facilities was essential in order to make effective and reliable future estimates. Data had been accumulated on staff, space, and equipment needs (Figure 4.15), as well as information concerning spatial proximity, or who should be placed where. The underlying premise for accommodating people in an organizational situation is that physical nearness should be related to the amount of communication that takes place between them. Surveys were developed to identify interaction patterns, where individuals recorded daily communication with every other person in the organization (Figure 4.17). Simplified surveys can also be developed to minimize the amount of data collected by reducing a large organization to smaller groups, such as departments. It is also possible to replace numerical counts of communication by estimates of actual communication through the use of an office questionnaire, which establishes an approximation of the inter-personal structure and communication patterns of an organization. Individual interviews, by contrast, are more time consuming and generally yield qualitative information that takes longer to analyze. Combinations of the two methods can generally provide a considerable amount of useful information. And finally, there is no substitute for going to the organization and observing everyone at their tasks.

From the results of the questionnaire, it was evident that the fulfillment of the organization's objectives was achieved through the development of project teams. The duration of the team's efforts varied with outside funding, and usually lasted between one and two years. A summary of all questionnaire data was compiled for each staff member which provided the staff and the designer with a basic description of the organization. Additional data was collected through an activity description survey where staff described their individual roles, responsibilities, and requirements (Figure 4.16).

The office staff work profile (Figure 4.17) described the nature and extent of communication within the organization. Personal relationships and priorities within the agency, and the frequency and nature of contact with the public were recorded by each individual. This profile and the communications analysis diagrams (Figure 4.18) contributed to the development of the socio - physical organizational diagram (Figure 4.19). The communications

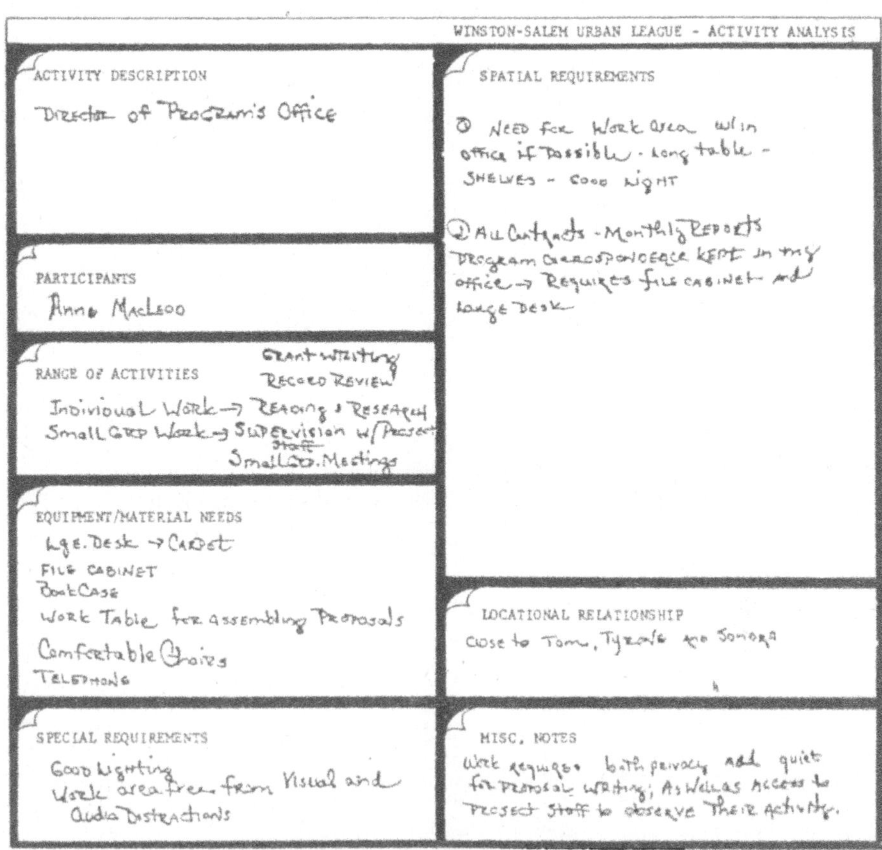

WINSTON-SALEM URBAN LEAGUE - ACTIVITY ANALYSIS

ACTIVITY DESCRIPTION

Director of Program's Office

PARTICIPANTS

Anne MacLeod

RANGE OF ACTIVITIES

Individual Work → Reading & Research, Grant writing, Record Review

Small Grp Work → Supervision w/Project Staff, Small Grp. Meetings

EQUIPMENT/MATERIAL NEEDS

Lge. Desk → Carpet

File Cabinet

Book Case

Work Table for assembling Proposals

Comfortable Chairs

Telephone

SPECIAL REQUIREMENTS

Good Lighting

Work area free from Visual and Audio Distractions

SPATIAL REQUIREMENTS

① Need for Work area w/in office if possible - long table - shelves - good light

② All Contracts - Monthly Reports Program correspondence kept in my office → Requires file cabinet and large Desk

LOCATIONAL RELATIONSHIP

Close to Tom, Tyrone and Sonora

MISC. NOTES

Work requires both privacy and quiet for proposal writing; As well as access to project staff to observe their activity.

Figure 4.16 Activity description form

Office staff	Individual work: Frequency (Not at all / Little / Half time / Often / Always); Percentage (%) (Reading / Report writing / Phoning / Other)	Description	Communication: Personal (In your office / In their office / Both); Memo; Interoffice memo; Telephone	Outside contact: 1 on 1 (Often / Sometimes / Never); Group (Often / Sometimes / Never); Duration (Less than 1/2 hour / 1/2 hour / More than 1 hour)	Privacy: Audial (Often / Sometimes / Never); Visual (Often / Sometimes / Never)
1. Tyrone Posey		administrating (50%)			
2. Anne McLeod		supervising (20%)			
3. Sondra Pennington		assisting & supervising (90%)			
4. Hazel Brown		n.a.			
5. Deborah King		n.a.			
6. Rhonda Jones		counseling (95%)			
7. Carolyn Hackney		counseling (40%)			
8. Jonis Grayson		counseling (40%)			
9. Marilyn Rich		field work (25%)			
10. Sarah Coleman		counseling (40%)			
11. G. J. Sadler		administration (65%)			
12. Gary Henderson		counseling (25%)			
13. Lassiter		in seminars (20%)			

Figure 4.17 Office staff work profile

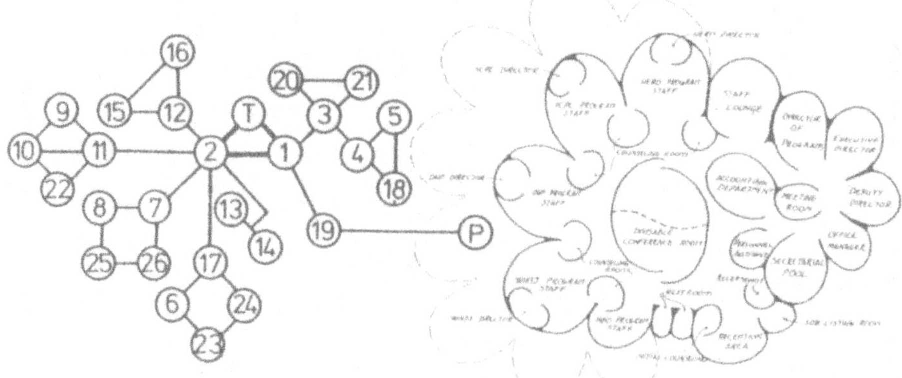

Figure 4.18 Communications analysis diagram: Office sociogram

Figure 4.20 Relationship diagram corresponding to sociogram

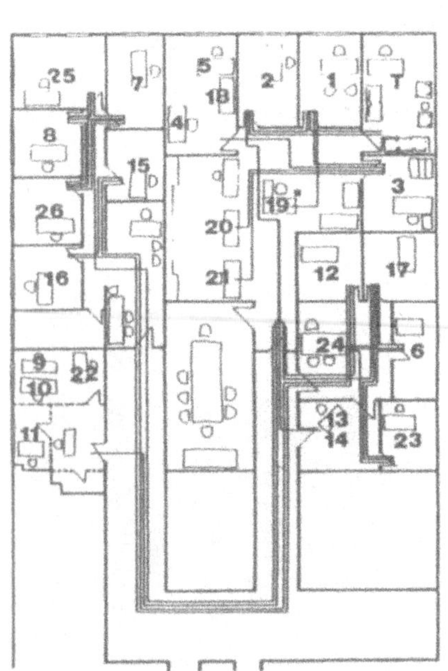

Figure 4.19 Plan of exisiting offices showing communications links

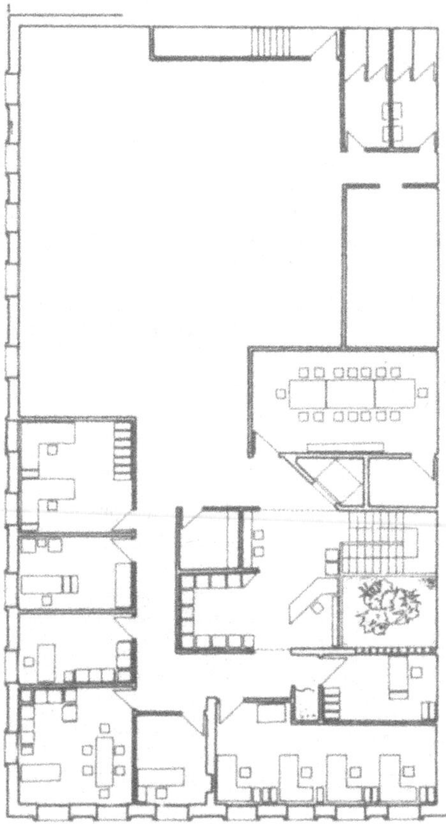

Figure 4.21 Plan of proposed office layout

network diagram (Figure 4.18) summarized the working interrelationship between staff members which subsequently served as a guide for achieving the desired spatial adjacencies. These data were also derived from questions pertaining to work interactions. Other communications diagrams were developed from staff responses to informal office contacts and personal preferences. Each of the diagrams were either compiled into a summary diagram or analyzed independently.

Spatial requirements were arrived at from space standards, information contained in the activity descriptions, and an evaluation of existing space use according to such criteria as privacy, accessibility, comfort, and illumination. These assessments were conducted with the occupants of each area, and a member of the design team (Figure 4.20).

Although the intent of this example is to describe a procedure for self-assessment, the first step in the programming process, it is often desirable to transform the results of such an inquiry into a plan of action. To this end, a diagram for reorganizing staff members locations further helped to clarify the links identified in the communcations network diagram (Figure 4.18). This diagram was useful in facilitating discussions with members of the organization, and established a point at which final agreement could be achieved prior to developing floor plan arrangements. The final plan achieved consensus since it resulted from a comparative analysis of each existing space to the desired arrangement (Figure 4.21) where all staff members were able to contribute to the development of their own work spaces.

Acknowledgment

This project was conducted by Steven Clipp and Mete Gurel, under the direction of Henry Sanoff, Director, Community Development Group, School of Design, North Carolina State University. An earlier version appeared in *Design Studies,* 6, 4 (1985): 181-186.

Conclusion

There are many benefits accruing from a Theory Z-action approach, for the community, the users, and the architects. Firstly, from the social point of view, integrating research, practice, and participation can result in a greater meeting of social needs and an increasingly effective utilization of resources at the disposal of a particular community (Cashden, Fahle, Francis, Schwartz, and Stein, 1978). Secondly, to the user group, it represents an increased sense of having influenced the design decision-making process and an increased awareness of the consequences of decisions made. Thirdly, to the architect, it represents more relevant and up-to-date information than was possible before (Sanoff, 1988). Increasingly, architects have described their participatory experiences as rewarding and influential in changing their relationship with clients and users (Burns, 1983; Kaplan McLaughlin, 1981; and Lewis and Gindroz, 1974).

Clearly, this suggests an expanded role for the professional to include the function of instructor, and facilitator of the design process, in addition to being an advocate for the principles of architecture. Practitioners can easily change their behavior to accomodate this new role. It requires a shift in the allocation of time from design development to the front end or pre-design stage where more reliable information input can minimize the time normally wasted in second guessing client needs, requirements, and preferences. This new role will subsequently increase the architect's social standing, esteem, and respect in the community. A process that is rooted in open and meaningful communication is essential to learning. Through mutual learning changes can be brought about. These changes will evolve since it may no longer be necessary to produce finished and unalterable solutions, but to extract solutions from a continuous dialogue with those who will use the architect's work.

The implications for educating Theory Z designers are challenging since the involvement of clients/users or their surrogates suggests the need for face to face contact, collaboration, and learning how to listen and how to observe. The designer can be trained to observe objectively, to replicate occasions, and to sample situations and individuals (Lawton, 1981). It requires the development of communication skills and tools that facilitate understanding, particularly since the client constituency cannot comprehend the architects language. This dos not suggest an abrogation of the architects responsibilities. Rather, as the case studies attempt to illustrate, a willingness for user groups to accept new ideas, and to defer to the architects expertise especially when they have experienced the types of decisions normally made by design professionals. Designing within the context of the client/user also provides students with the opportunity to develop their verbal abilities which constitutes a basic communication requirement. The process of making the decision process transparent will inadvertently impact on student's ability to control the quality of their work as well as to increase people's general level of awareness of design issues.

References

Abt, C. (1970), *Serious Games*, Viking Press, New York.

Albrecht, J. (1988), 'Towards a theory of participation in architecture - An examination of humanistic planning theories', *Journal of Architectural Education*, 42,1:24-31.

Alexander, C. (1972), *The Oregon Experiment*, Oxford University Press, New York.

Alexander, C., Ishikawa, S. & Silverstein, M. (1977), *A Pattern Language: Towns, Buildings, Constructions*, Oxford University Press, New York.

Arnstein, S. (1969), 'A ladder of citizen participation', *Journal of the American Institute of Planners*, 35:215-24.

Bechtel, R.B, Marans, R.W. & Michelson, W. (1987), *Methods in Environmental and Behavioral Research*, Van Nostrand Reinhold, New York.

Becker, F. (1977), *Housing Messages*, Dowden Hutchinson & Ross, Stroudsburg, Pennsylvania.

Becker, F. (1981), *Workspace: Creating Environments in Organizations*. Praeger, New York.

Bennis, W. (1966), *Changing Organizations*, McGraw Hill, New York.

Bettelheim, B. (1974), *Home for the Heart*, Bantam, New York.

Bishop, J. (1977), 'CRIG Analysis', *Bulletin of Environmental Education* , 73:3-8.

Blau, P.M. & Scott, W.R. (1962),*Formal Organizations*, Chandler Publishing, San Francisco, California.

Brill, M. & BOSTI (1984), *Using Office Design to Increase Productivity,Vol.1*, Workplace Design and Productivity, Inc., Buffalo, New York.

Building Research Board. (1986), *Programming Practices in the Building Process: Opportunities for Improvement,* National Academy Press, Washington, DC.

Burke, E.M. (1968), 'Citizen participation strategies', *Journal of the American Institute of Planners,* 34,5:287-294.

Burns, J. (1979), *Connections: Ways to Discover and Realize Community Potentials,* McGraw Hill, New York.

Burns, J. (1983), 'Designing for (and with) the Christian Brothers: A participatory planning process is taken in two stages', *American Institute of Architects Journal,* 72:60-63.

Canter, D. (1970), 'Should we treat building users as subjects or objects'? in Canter, D. (ed.), *Architectural Psychology,* RIBA Publications, London.

Canter, D. & Thorne, R. (1976). 'Attitudes to housing: A cross cultural comparison', *Environment & Behavior,* 8:239-264.

Canty, D. (1976). Editorial. *Journal of the American Institute of Architects,* August.

Cashden, L., Fahle, B., Francis, M., Schwartz, S. & Stein, S. (1978), 'A critical framework for participatory approaches to environmental change', in Francis, M. (ed.), *Participatory Planning and Neighborhood Control.* Center for Human Environments, City University of New York.

Cohen, U., Hill, A.H., Lane, C.G. McGinty,T. & Moore, G.T. (1989), *Recommendations for Child Play Areas,* University of Wisconsin, Center for Architecture & Urban Planning Research, Milwaukee. .

Cohen, U., Moore, G.T. & McGinty, T. (1978), *Case Studies of Child Play Areas and Support Facilities,* University of Wisconsin, Center for Architecture & Urban Planning, Milwaukee.

Cooper-Marcus, C. & Sarkissian, W. (1986), *Housing as if People Mattered,* University of California Press, Berkeley, California.

Craik, K.H. (1968), 'The comprehension of the everyday physical environment', *Journal of the American Institute of Planners,* 34,1:29-37.

Craik, K.H. & Zube, E.H. (1976), *Perceiving Environmental Quality: Research and Applications,* Plenum, New York.

Craik, K.H. & McKechnie, G.E. (1974), *Perception of Environmental Quality: Preferential Judgements versus Comparative Appraisals,* Unpublished manuscript, University of California, Berkeley, California.

Cunningham, B. (1976), 'Action research: Toward a procedural model', *Human Relations,* 29,215-238.

Daish, J.R., Gray, J., Kernohan, D. & Salmond, A. (1982), 'Post-occupancy evaluation in New Zealand', *Design Studies,* 3,2.

Daniel,T.C. & Boster, R.S. (1976), 'Measuring landscape aesthetics: The Scenic Beauty Estimation method', (Research paper RM-167), US Department of Agriculture, Rocky Mountain Forest and Ranger Experiment Station, Fort Collins, Colorado.

Davidoff, P. (1965), 'Advocacy and pluralism in planning', *Journal of the American Institute of Planning,* 31:331-38

Davis, G. (1978), 'A process for adapting existing buildings for new offices', in Preiser, W.F.E. (ed.),*Facility Programming,* Dowden Hutchinson & Ross, Stroudsburg, Pennsylvania.

Davis, G. & Szigeti, F. (1979), 'Functional & technical programming, when the owner/ sponsor is a large or complex organization', in Simon, J.G. (ed.), *Conflicting Experiences of Space,* Proceedings of the Fourth International Architectural Psychology Conference, Catholic Universty of Louvain, Belgium.

Davis, G. & Szigeti, F. (1986), 'Planning and programming offices: Determining user requirements', in Wineman, J.D. (ed.), *Behavioral Issues in Office Design,* Van Nostrand Reinhold, New York.

Davis, S. (1981). *Close Encounters with the Built Environment,* Evergreen Press, Canada.

Delbecq, A.L., van der Ven, & Gustafson, D.H. (1975), *Group Techniques for Program Planning,* Scott Foresman, Glen View, Illinois.

Dorman, G. (1981),*Middle Grades Assessment Program,* Center for Early Adolescence, University of North Carolina, Chapel Hill.

Downs, A. (1976), *Urban Problems and Prospects,* Markham, Chicago.

Drucker (1968), *The Practice of Management,* Pan Books, London.

Ellsworth, M.E.B. & Leonard, J. (1988), 'Working together: Administrators and the campus care director', in Keyes, C.R. & Cook, R.E. (eds.), *Campus Child Care Issues and Practices,* National Coalition for Campus Child Care, Inc., Milwaukee.

Farbstein, J.D. (1985), 'Using the program: Applications for design, occupancy, and evaluation', in Preiser, W.F.E. (ed.), *Programming the Built Environment,* Van Nostrand Reinhold, New York.

Field, T.M. (1980), 'Preschool play: Effects of teacher/child ratios and organization of classroom space', *Child Study Journal,* 10,3:191-205.

Francescato, G., Weidemann, S., Anderson, J.R. & Chenoweth, R. (1980), *Residents' Satisfaction in HUD-Assisted Housing: Design and Management factors,* US Government Printing Office, Washington, DC.

Freidman, A. Zimring, C. & Zube, E. (1978), *Environmental Design Evaluation,* Plenum, New York.

Frost, J.L. & Klein, B.L. (1983). *Children's Play and Playgrounds,* Playscapes, Austin, Texas.

Godschalk, D. (1972), *Participation, Planning, and Exchange in Old and New Communities: A Collaborative Paradigm,* University of North Carolina, Chapel Hill.

Gordon, J.J. (1961), *Synectics:The Development of Creative Capacity,* Collier, New York.

Gould, B.P. (1986), 'Facilities programming', in Braybrooke, S. (ed.), *Design for Research,* Wiley, New York.

Gray, J., Watson, C.G., Daish, J.R. & Kernohan, D. (1985), 'Putting a POE to work: A case study in which a POE is combined with participatory programming', in Klein, S., Wener, R. & Lehman, E.S. (eds.), *Environmental Change/ Social Change,* Environmental Design Research Association, Washington, DC.

Habraken, J. (1986), 'Towards a new professional role', *Design Studies,* 7,3: 139

Halprin, L. & Burns, J. (1974),*Taking Part: A Workshop Approach to Collective Creativity,* MIT Press, Cambridge.

Hancock, W. (1977), 'Quality, productivity, and workplace design: An engineering perspective, *Journal of Contemporary Business,* 11,2:107-11

Hertzberg, F., Mausner, R. & Snyderman, B.B. (1959), *The Motivation to Work*, Wiley, New York.

Hinrichs, C.L. (1985), 'Designing the design coalition team: Owner/user particiption in Architecture', *Design Coalition Team*, Proceedings of the International Design Participation Conference, Eindoven, Holland.

Hunt, M.E. (1985), 'Enhancing a building's imageability', *Journal of Architectural & Planning Research*, 2:151-168.

Jencks, C. (1971), *Architecture 2000: Prediction and Methods*, Praeger, New York .

Jones, J.C. (1970), *Design Methods: Seeds of Human Futures*, Wiley, London.

Kaplan, S. (1979), 'Perception and landscape: Conceptions and misconceptions', in Elsner, G.H. & Smardon, R.C. (eds.), Our National Landscape, pp.241-48. USDA Forest Service, General Technical Report, PSW-35. Berkeley, California.

Kaplan/Mclaughlin (1981), 'Feasibility study and program guide for a health clinic', in Palmer, M. (ed.),*The Architects Guide to Facility Programming*, McGraw Hill, New York.

Katz, R.L. (1960), 'Toward a more effective enterprise', *Harvard Business Review*, 38,5:80-112.

Katzell, R., Bienstock, P. & Farbstein, P. (1975), *A Guide to Worker Productivity Experiments in the United States 1971-1975*, New York University Press, New York.

Kelly, J. (1955), *The Psychology of Personal Constructs*, Norton, New York.

Krampen, M. (1979), *Meaning in the Urban Environment*, Pion, London.

Kritchevsky, S., Prescott, E. & Walling, L. (1974), 'Planning environments for young children: Physical space', in Coates, G. (ed.), *Alternative Learning Environments*, Hutchinson & Ross, Stroudsburg, Pennsylvania.

Kurtz, J. H. (1978), 'Habitable schools: Programming for a changing environment', in Preiser, W.F.E. (ed.), *Facility Programming*, Van Nostrand Reinhold, New York.

Lawton, P. (1981), 'Sensory deprivation and the effect of the environment on management of the patient with senile dementia', in Miller, N. & Cohen, G. (eds.), *Clinical Aspects Alzheimer's Disease and Senile Dementia*, Raven Press, New York.

Lewin, K. (1946), 'Action research and minority problems', *Journal of Social Issues*, 2:34-36.

Lewin, K. Lippitt, R. & White, R. (1939), 'Patterns of aggressive behavior in experimentally created social climates', *Journal of Social Psychology*, 10: 271-299.

Lewis, D. & R. Gindroz (1974), 'Toward a design process that re-enfranchises citizens and consumers', *American Institute of Architects Journal* , 62, 5:28-31.

Likert, R. (1967), *The Human Organization: Its Management and Value*, McGraw Hill, New York.

Litton, R.B. (1968), *Forest Landscape Description and Inventories*, USDA Forest Service, Research Paper PSW-49, Berkeley, California.

Low, S.M. (1987), 'Developments in research design, data collection, and analysis: Qualitative methods', in Zube, E.H. & Moore, G.T. (eds.), *Advances in Environment, Behavior, and Design*, Vol.1, Plenum, New York.

Marans, R. & Ahrentzen, S. (1987), 'Developments in research design, data collection, and analysis: Quantitative methods', in Zube, E.H. & Moore, G.T. (eds.), *Advances in Environment, Behavior, and Design*, Vol.1. Plenum, New York.

Marans, R. W. & Spreckelmeyer, K.F. (1981), *Evaluating Built Environments: A Behavioral Approach*, Institute for Social Research, Ann Arbor, Michigan.

McGregor, D. (1960), *The Human Side of Enterprise*, McGraw Hill, New York.

McLaughlin, H. (1976), 'Programming', in Class, R.A. & Koehler, R.E. (eds.), *Curent Techniques in Architectural Practice*, American Institute of Architects and Architectural Record, Washington, DC & New York.

Michelson, W. (1975), *Behavioral Research Methods in Environmental Design*, Hutchinson & Ross, Stroudsburg, Pennsylvania.

Moleski, W. (1971), 'Behavioral analysis and environmental programming for offices', in Lang, J., Burnette, C., Moleski, W. & Vachon, D. (eds.), *Designing for Human Behavior: Architecture and the Behavioral Sciences*, Dowden Hutchinson & Ross, Stroudsburg, Pennsylvania.

Moore, G.T. (1986), Effects of the spatial definition of behavior settings on children's behavior: 'A quasi-experimental field study', *Journal of Environmental Psychology*, 6:205-231.

Moore, G.T. (1987), 'The physical environment and cognitive development in child care centers', in Weinstein, C.S. & David, T.G. (eds.), *Spaces for Children: The Built Environment & Child Development*, Plenum, New York.

Moore, G.T., Lane, C.G. Hill, A.H., Cohen, U. & McGinty, T. (1989), *Recommendations for Child Care Centers*. University of Wisconsin, Center for Architecture & Planning Research, Milwaukee.

Moreno, J. (1934), *Who Shall Survive?* Beacon House, New York.

Newman, O. (1973), *Defensible Space*, Collier, New York.

Oberdorfer, J. (1988), 'Community participation in the design of the Boulder Creek Branch Library', *Design Studies*, 9,1:4-13.

Osgood, C., Suci, G. & Tannenbaum, P. (1957), *The Measurement of Meaning*, University of Illinois Press, Urbana.

Ouchi, W. (1981), *Theory Z: How American Business Can Meet the Japanese Challenge*, Addison-Wesley, Reading, Massachusetts.

Palmer, M. (1981), *The Architect's Guide to Facility Programming*, American Institute of Architects and Architectural Record, Washington, DC and New York.

Pena, W. (1977), *Problem Seeking: An Architectural Programming Primer*, Cahners Books, Boston.

Pitt, D.G. & Zube, E.H. (1979),The Q-sort method: Use in landscape assessment research and landscape planning, in Elsner, G.H. & Smardon, R.C. (eds.), *Our National Landscape*, USDA Forest Service, General Technical Report, PSW-35, Berkeley, California.

Porter, L., Lawler, E. & Hackman, J. (1975), *Behavior in Organizations*, McGraw Hill, New York.

Preiser, W.F.E. (1978), *Facility Programming*, Van Nostrand Reinhold, New York.

Preiser, W.F.E. (1985), *Programming the Built Environment*, Van Nostrand Reinhold, New York.

Preiser, W.F.E., Rabinowitz, H.Z. & White, E.T. (1988), *Post-Occupancy Evaluation,* Van Nostrand Reinhold, New York.

Preiser, W.F.E. (1992), *Professional Practice in Facility Programming,* Van Nostrand Reinhold, New York.

Prescott, E., Jones, E., Kritcchevsky, C., Milich, C. & Haselhoef, E. (1976), *Assessments of Child Rearing Environments: An Ecological Approach,* Pacific Oaks College, Pasadena, CA.

Prescott, E. & David, T.G. (1976), 'The effects of the physical environment in child care systems', Concept paper, Pacific Oaks College, Pasadena, CA.

Proshansky, H.M., Ittelson, W.H. & Rivlin, L.G. (1976), *Environmental Psychology, 2nd Edition: People and their Physical Settings,* Holt, Rinehart and Winston, New York.

Rainwater, L. (1956), 'Fear and the house-as-haven in the lower class', *Journal of the American Institute of Planners,* 32:23-37.

Riland, L.H. (1970), Summary: A resurvey of employee reactions to the landscape environment one year after initial occupation, *Eastman Kodak,* Rochester, New York.

Robinson, J. & Weeks, S. (1984), *Programming as Design,* University of Minnesota, School of Architecture, Minneapolis.

Rohe, W. & Nuffer, E. (1977), 'The effects of density and partitioning on children's behavior', Paper presented at the 85th Annual meeting, American Psychological Association, San Francisco, CA.(mimeo).

Rosner, J. (1978), 'Matching method to purpose: The challenges of planning citizen participation activities', in Langton, S. (ed.), *Citizen Participation in America,* Lexington Books, New York.

Ruesh, J. & Kees, W. (1956), *Non-Verbal Communication: Notes on the Visual Perception of Human Relations,* University of California, Berkeley, California.

Sanoff, H. (1977), *Methods of Architectural Programming,* Van Nostrand Reinhold, New York.

Sanoff, H. (1981), 'User needs program for a research facility', *Design Studies,* 6,4:187-195.

Sanoff, H, (1983), *Planning Outdoor Play,* Humanics, Atlanta, Georgia.

Sanoff, H. (1984), *Arts Center Workbook,* North Carolina Arts Council and North Carolina State University, School of Design, Raleigh, NC.

Sanoff, H. (1988), 'Participatory design in focus', *Architecture and Behavior,* 4,1:27-42.

Sanoff, H. (1989), 'Facility programming', in Zube, E.H. & Moore, G.T. (eds.), *Advances in Environment, Behavior, and Design,* Vol.2, Plenum, New York.

Sanoff, H. (1991). *Visual Research Methods in Design,* Van Nostrand Reinhold, New York.

Sanoff, H. & Sanoff, J. (1988), *Learning Environments for Children,* Humanics, Atlanta, Georgia.

Seidel. A. (1982), 'Usable E.B.R.: What can we learn from other fields'? in Bart, P., Chen, A. & Francescato, G. (eds.), *Knowledge for Design,* Environmental Design Research Association, Washington, DC.

Schein, E.H. (1969), *Process Consultation,* Addison-Wesley, Reading, MA.

Silver, G.H. & Klein, R.A. (1985), 'Get your space act together', *Office Systems'85,* Springhouse Corporation, Springhouse, Pennsylvania.

Smith, P.K. & Connolly, K.J. (1980), *The Ecology of Preschool Behavior*, Cambridge University, Cambridge, England.

Sommer, R. (1979), 'Participatory design', *Ideas*, Herman Miller, Ann Arbor, Michigan.

Spreckelmeyer, K. (1987), 'Environmental programming', in Bechtel, R.B., Marans, R.W. & Michelson, W. (eds.), *Methods in Environmental and Behavioral Research*, Van Nostrand Reinhold, New York.

Susman, G. & R. Evered (1978), 'An assessment of the scientific merits of action research', *Administrative Science Quarterly*, 23:582-603.

Taylor, J.G., Zube, E.H. & Sell, J.L. (1987), 'Landscape assessment and perception research methods', in Bechtel, R.B., Marans, R.W. & Michelson, W. (eds.), *Methods of Environmental and Behavioral Research*, Van Nostrand Reinhold, New York.

Threlfall, M. (1986), 'Inside/outside: The school environment', *Children's Environment Quarterly*, 3,3:30-39.

Tusler, W.H., Schraisahuhn, R.T. & Meyer, E.R. (1985), 'Stone, Marraccini and Patterson's health care facility programming', in Preiser, W.F.E. (ed.), *Programming the Built Environment*, Van Nostrand Reinhold, New York.

Verba, S. (1961), *Small Groups and Political Behavior: A Study of Leadership*, Princeton University Press, Princeton, New Jersey.

Warren, R.L. (1965), *Types of Purposive Social Change at the Community Level*, No.11, Papers in Social Welfare, Brandeis University, Waltham, Massachusetts.

Weinstein, C.S. (1987), 'Designing preschool classrooms to support development', in Weinstein, C.S. & David, T.G. (eds.), *Spaces for Children: The Built Environment and Child Development.*, Plenum, New York.

Wells, B. (1972), 'The psycho-social influence of building environments: Sociometric findings in large and small office spaces', in Gutman, R. (ed.),*People and Buildings*, Basic Books, New York.

Weisman, G.D. (1983), 'Environmental programming and action research', *Environment and Behavior*, 15, 381-408

Wener, R. (1989), 'Environmental evaluation', in Zube, E.H. & Moore, G.T. (eds.), *Advances in Environment, Behavior, and Design*, Vol. 2, Plenum, New York.

White, E.T. (1972), *Introduction to Architectural Programming*, Architectural Media, Tuscon, Arizona.

White, E.T. (1982), *Interviews with Architects about Facility Programming*, Florida A&M University, Tallahassee, Florida.

White, E.T. (1983), *Project Programming: A Growing Architectural Service*, Florida A&M University, Tallahasse, Florida.

Willems, E. (1973), 'Place and motivation: Independence and complexity in patient behavior', in Mitchell, W. (ed.), *EDRA-3: Proceedings from the 3rd Annual Environmental Design Research Association Conference*, 4,3:11-8. Los Angeles, California.

Wineman, J. (1982), 'Office design and evaluation', *Environment and Behavior*, 14:271-298.

Wolwhill, J.F. & Kohn, I. (1976), 'Dimensionalizing the environmental manifold', in Wapner, S., Kaplan, B. & Cohn, S.B. (eds.), *Experiencing the Environment*, Plenium, New York.

Wrona, S. (1981), *Participation in Architectural Design and Urban Planning*, Warsaw Polytechnic, Poland.

Wulz, F. (1986), 'The concept of participation', *Design Studies*, 7,3:153-62.

Zeisel, J. (1981), *Inquiry by Design*, Brooks/Cole, Belmont, California.

Zetlin, L.R. (1969), *A Comparison of Employee Attitudes Toward the Conventional and Landscape Office*, Report to Organization and Procedures Department, Port of New York Authority, New York.

Zimring, C. & Reizenstein, J.E. (1981), 'A primer on post-occupancy evaluation', *American Institute of Architects Journal*, 70,13:52-58.

Index